COOKING WITH CARIBBEAN RUM

Laurel-Ann Morley

D1401140

MACMILLAN
CARIBBEAN

First published 1991 by
MACMILLAN EDUCATION LTD
London and Oxford
Companies and representatives throughout the world

www.macmillan-caribbean.com

ISBN 0–333–54558–3

15   14   13   12   11   10   9   8   7   6
10   09   08   07   06   05   04   03   02   01

This book is printed on paper suitable for recycling and
made from fully managed and sustained forest sources.

Printed in China

A catalogue record for this book is available from the
British Library.

Cover photographs Felix Kerr

CONTENTS

Foreword   5

About rum   7

Measurements   8

Drinks   11

Soups and starters   15

Poultry   19

Beef and lamb   33

Pork   39

Fish   47

Stuffings and vegetables   55

Desserts   59

Cakes, pastries and sauces   71

Index   79

FOREWORD

I was born in Venezuela, South America, but have lived in Barbados since I was ten years old and there is no doubt that Barbados is home!

I am not a professional home economist but a housewife who honestly enjoys cooking. I have done so since I was a child (thanks to my mother who taught me and encouraged me through the years).

I have travelled extensively, visiting England, Europe, Greece, India, Singapore, Bangkok, Hong Kong, Japan, Australia, New Zealand, Hawaii, USA, Mexico, Peru, Bolivia and, naturally, many of the Caribbean Islands and I have always insisted on eating only the local foods. After these visits I have enjoyed returning home and entertaining friends with a meal consisting entirely of the specialities of the country I have been to. — 'It's Indonesian Night' — 'It's Mexican Night' — 'It's Indian Night at the Morleys' — so go the invitations.

I spent a year working with one of our leading delicatessens where I learnt a lot about mass producing food and cake icing, and was lucky enough to be given a free hand in trying out new items to bring out for sale.

I have cooked and helped with many weddings, twenty-firsts, business parties and special occasion parties where I specialise in coming up with cocktail snacks with a difference. In some cases I have even decorated the premises with a particular theme to suit the food. My most memorable of these are:

- 'Valentines Night' – 120 guests – a red and white night where I designed everything from the invitations to the cupids' hearts that hung on the walls; I even made red heart shapes to use as place mats for the food.

- 'Mexican Night' – 75 guests – I took down all the paintings from the walls and put up Mexican sombreros, donkeys, cacti etc. Naturally, Mexican food was served to Mariachi music and the staff wore Mexican outfits.

- 'Indonesian Night' – 40 guests to a sit-down 14-course meal – the plates consisted of coconut and pineapple shells and banana leaves, and the place mats were breadfruit leaves. The entire house was decorated with thousands of hibiscus flowers and naturally the staff wore sarongs to go along with the theme.

- 'Tropical garden night' – 160 guests – I decorated two outdoor tents with masses of Boston hanging ferns at different levels, sprinkled with tiny white lights to give a star effect. Naturally the food was barbecued outdoors so the aroma could add to the atmosphere.

Party food (opposite) – *reading clockwise,* Strawberry Mousse Cake *(top)*, Orange Chicken, and Seafood Crepes

So you see, my delight is not only in preparing the meals but also in creating the atmosphere to suit what I have so enjoyed preparing.

Years ago, my sister-in-law encouraged me to write a cook book and, with the assistance of Hanschell Inniss Ltd. – the blenders and bottlers of **Cockspur Rum**, the favourite golden rum of the Barbadians, for over 100 years – here it is! I should like to thank 'Cockspur' for their outstanding rum, which I have used in many of my recipes in this book.

Why cook with rum? Well, anyone who has visited the Caribbean will know that putting a little bit of rum into almost anything enhances the flavour. Besides, why not? In the Caribbean, and especially Barbados, we do produce some of the best rums in the world.

What I had in mind when writing this book was to make it as homely as possible. After all, few of us are home economists or food stylists. In many of the pictures the food was cooked by me and photographed by me. That was fun! Ask my neighbours and family who got to sample so many dishes because it was too much for just us to eat.

Naturally I could not end this without saying just a little something about Barbados. 'Barbados is different' – an opinion given by most visitors to our island, and so she is!

The island, although considered as being in the Caribbean is in fact entirely surrounded by the Atlantic Ocean, a hundred or so miles east of the Caribbean chain of islands. Unlike most of the neighbouring islands, it is a coral island, relatively flat, rising gradually in terraces to 1100 feet at its highest point. Barbados is blessed with an almost perfect climate and, because of the coral reefs that surround it, with some of the most beautiful white coral beaches to be found anywhere.

Barbados is the only West Indian island that has always been ruled by the British system. It was uninhabited, covered by dense forest, when the British settled in 1627. In 1966 Barbados became independent but remained a state within the Commonwealth and retains the Queen of England as the Queen of Barbados.

Barbados is 21 miles long by 14 miles wide. The Atlantic sides (north and east) are rugged and picturesque with large Atlantic breakers pounding the beaches, while on the west side the sea is calm and tranquil, ideal for sea bathing.

The climate boasts bright sunshine for most of the year, with temperatures of 22° – 30° Celsius. Although tropical, the island is blessed with a constant sea breeze which cools her down.

The capital of Barbados is Bridgetown which houses the commercial centre and the home of Parliament.

The language spoken is English – with a very distinctive way of speaking known as *bajan* – so come visit and enjoy some West Indian cooking.

Cockspur Rum is available in several of the Caribbean islands, and is also exported to USA, Canada, Australia, Great Britain and Germany.

ABOUT RUM

Rum is a spirit, as are whisky, gin and vodka. Rum is obtained from distilling either the juice extracted from the sugar cane or, more often, from molasses, which is the brown syrup left over after the sugar is extracted from the sugar cane juice.

Rum, in some form or another, may have been distilled as long as 2000 years ago. Christopher Columbus introduced sugar cane to the West Indies and, from the sixteenth century, sugar was produced on a large scale throughout the Caribbean.

Naturally, as I live in Barbados, I shall describe the history of rum there. Barbados was not the first country to distill rum but it was almost certainly the country where the name 'rum' came from, and one of the first countries to export rum.

By the end of the nineteenth century all Barbados rum was made by individual sugar plantations, in their own stills, adjacent to their sugar mills. Today, rum is distilled by independent rum refineries. All rum is white when distilled. It is put into oak barrels to age and takes colour from the wood. As the intensity of the colour can vary from barrel to barrel and change according to the length of time it is aged, most dealers add a small amount of caramel to ensure uniformity in colour.

Barbados rum is sold in two colours, the white or 'see through' as it is known locally, and the beautiful golden rum which is more popular with the locals. If you know your rums from around the world you will find that, although they are all basically distilled in the same manner, each country produces a flavour all of its own. Why this is so no one knows, but Barbados rum is, in my personal opinion, the very best that can be obtained. Perhaps what makes the difference is the water, soil and climate of each individual country and certainly Barbados enjoys the best of these ideal conditions.

Some of the better known brands of Caribbean rum are Cockspur, Alleyne Arthur and Mount Gay.

(Information taken from *The Barbados Rum Book,* published by Macmillan Publishers Ltd 1985)

MEASUREMENTS

Measurements given in this book are imperial and metric. Cups used are standard American cups.

1 lb = 0.4536 kg	1 kg = 1000 g
1 oz = 28.35 g	= 2.2046 lb
1 pt = 0.5683 ℓ	1 g = 0.0353 oz
	1 ℓ = 1000 mℓ
	= 35 fl oz

There is no direct conversion from pounds (lb) to grams (g), or from pints (pt) to litres (ℓ), so the following approximations have been used.

1 oz = 25 g
8 oz = 225 g
1 lb = 450 g

1 pt = 20 fl oz = 600 mℓ
1 fl oz = 30 mℓ
1 gallon (gall) = 8 pt = 5 ℓ

1 pt = 2½ cups
1 cup = 8 fl oz = 240 mℓ

For any recipe, use only imperial or only metric measurements throughout.

Oven temperatures

Fahrenheit	Centigrade	Gas mark
250°	120°	½
275°	140°	1
300°	150°	2
325°	175°	3
350°	180°	4
375°	190°	5
400°	200°	6
425°	215°	7
450°	230°	8
475°	250°	9
500°	260°	

RECIPES

Simple Spareribs

DRINKS

Party Punch

Mexican Coffee

½ cup strong brewed coffee
1 ½ tsp sugar
2 oz (50 g) semi-sweet chocolate, chopped
Pinch ground cinnamon
1 cup heated milk
2 tbsp rum
¼ cup sweetened whipped cream
Cinnamon

Heat the coffee and sugar in a heavy small saucepan, over a low heat, until the sugar is dissolved. Add the chocolate and a small pinch of cinnamon, and stir until the sugar is dissolved and the chocolate melts. Add the milk and whisk until frothy. Pour into mugs. Add 1 tablespoon of rum to each mug. Top with whipped cream and dust lightly with additional cinnamon.
Serves 2

Coconut Punch

1 26 fl oz (75 cl) bottle of white rum
2 dry coconuts, grated
1 cup granulated sugar
1 tsp vanilla extract
1 match

Combine the grated coconut and rum in a blender, blend for 2 minutes then strain the liquid through a cloth or fine sieve into a saucepan. Add the sugar to the saucepan and bring to the boil. Count 2 seconds from the boiling point, then ignite with the match. After a further 10 seconds, cover the saucepan to put out the flames. Allow to cool, stir in the vanilla and refrigerate. Stir well to blend before serving in wine glasses filled with crushed ice.
Serves 8 – 10

Make Ahead Party Punch

1 ½ cups sugar
2 cups lime juice
8 cups dry white wine
½ gallon (2 ½ ℓ) rum
1 cup maraschino cherries
2 cups diced pineapple
Angostura bitters to taste

Mix all the ingredients in a large bowl, stirring until the sugar is dissolved. Refrigerate overnight to combine flavours. Serve in punch bowls filled with crushed ice.
Serves 20 – 25

Ponche Crema

1 tin condensed milk
1 cup rum
6 eggs
1 tsp vanilla extract
Few drops lime juice
Angostura bitters
Freshly grated nutmeg

Combine the first five ingredients in a blender. Pour into glasses filled with crushed ice. Sprinkle a couple of drops of bitters on top, then garnish with grated nutmeg.
Serves 6

Poor Man's Liqueur

Do not let the name fool you, this is an easy, delicious, inexpensive and impressive after dinner liqueur to serve.

Pared rind from 2 – 3 limes cut in
  one continuous strip
2 cups rum
½ cup brown sugar

Place the pared lime rind in an ovenproof glass dish. Warm the rum in a saucepan. Pour the rum and sugar into the glass dish with the lime, ignite, stirring with a long spoon and lifting the flames for 2 – 3 minutes. Blow out flames and serve warm in liqueur glasses.
Serves 8 – 10

Hot Rum Mocha

¾ cup coffee liqueur
¼ cup creme de cacao
¼ cup orange flavoured liqueur
¼ cup rum
Hot strong brewed coffee
Frozen whipped dessert cream
  topping

Blend the first four ingredients in a jug.

To serve:
Pour 3 tablespoons liqueur and rum mixture into each mug. Add coffee, to within 1″ (2 cm) of the rim of the mug. Top with whipped topping and serve.
Serves 8 – 10

Coconut Punch

Orange Egg Nog

4 cups evaporated milk
4 eggs
¼ cup sugar
*1 6 oz (180 g) can frozen orange juice
   concentrate*
½ cup rum
¼ cup orange flavoured liqueur

Garnish:
Whipped topping
Ground nutmeg
Orange slices

Mix the first six ingredients in a blender until frothy. Pour into glasses filled with cracked ice and garnish with a dollop of whipped topping, a pinch of grated nutmeg and a slice of orange.
Serves 8

Spiced Milk Punch

¾ cup milk
¾ cup cream
6 tbsp creme de cacao
2 tbsp rum
4 tsp icing sugar
1 egg white

Garnish:
Chocolate shavings

Mix the first six ingredients in a blender until frothy. Serve immediately over crushed ice in stemmed glasses. Garnish with the chocolate.
Serves 4

SOUPS AND STARTERS

Orange Egg Nog *(top left)*, Coconut Punch *(top, centre)*, Rum-Nut Brie *(front, left)* and Cheddar-Rum Raisin Spread. Recipes for the Orange Egg Nog and the Coconut Punch are in the previous chapter.

Soy-Honey Drumettes

20 chicken wing drumettes
¼ cup soy sauce
¼ cup honey
1 tbsp vinegar
1 tbsp rum
2 tbsp freshly ground ginger

Put the chicken drumettes in a large bowl. Mix all the other ingredients together then pour over the chicken. Marinate the chicken drumettes in the mixture for 8 hours or over-night, turning frequently in the marinade.

Bake the drumettes in a preheated oven (400°F), turning and basting several times, for 30 – 40 minutes or until brown and glazed.
Serves 10 – 12 as cocktail snacks

Cheddar-Rum Raisin Spread

1 cup raisins
⅓ cup rum
8 oz (450 g) sharp Cheddar cheese, grated
8 oz (450 g) cream cheese, at room
  temperature
½ tsp curry powder
Dash hot pepper sauce

Soak the raisins in the rum for 1 hour. Use a slotted spoon to remove the raisins, set aside the raisins and the rum. Combine the cheeses in a medium bowl or food processor and mix until smooth and fluffy. Beat in the rum, curry powder and hot pepper sauce, then fold in the raisins. Pack tightly in a covered container. Refrigerate, to allow the flavours to blend, for up to 3 weeks.
Serves 8 – 10

Rum-Nut Brie

1½ tbsp brown sugar
1½ tbsp pecan or cashew nuts, chopped
2 tsp rum
1 4 oz (125 g) round Brie cheese
Crackers

Preheat the oven to 500°F.
Stir together the sugar, nuts and rum. Place the cheese on an ovenproof dish and bake in the oven for 4 – 5 minutes. Pile the sugar mixture over the top of the cheese. Bake for 2 – 3 minutes more or until the sugar melts. Serve with crackers.
Serves 6

Chicken Wings with Rum Barbecue Sauce

20 – 25 chicken wings
2 tbsp grated Parmesan cheese
¾ cup breadcrumbs
1 tsp paprika
½ tsp salt
⅓ cup cream or evaporated milk
½ cup butter

Combine the cheese, breadcrumbs, paprika and salt in a shallow bowl. Dip the chicken wings in the cream, coating them thoroughly, then roll them in the crumb mixture. Refrigerate for 1 hour to allow the coating to become firm.

Place the butter in a 13″ × 9″ × 2″ (33 cm × 23 cm × 5 cm) baking pan. Melt the butter in the oven as it heats to 375°F. Add the chicken pieces to the pan, turning them to coat in the butter. Bake for 40 minutes. Serve with **Rum Barbecue Sauce**, (page 17) either hot or cold.
Serves 12 – 15 as cocktail snacks

Rum Barbecue Sauce

2 tbsp oil
1 large onion, minced
2 cloves garlic, minced
1 cup bottled chilli sauce
⅓ cup lime juice
⅓ cup molasses
3 tbsp made mustard
1 tbsp Worcestershire sauce
¼ cup rum

Heat the oil in a medium saucepan, add the onion and garlic, cook for 2 minutes. Add all the remaining ingredients except the rum. Cover and simmer over a very low heat for 20 minutes. Remove from heat and stir in the rum.
Serves 12 – 15 with cocktail snacks

Carrot Soup with Coriander and Sour Cream

4 tbsp butter
½ cup finely chopped onions
3 cups finely chopped peeled carrots
3½ cups homemade or canned chicken broth
1 tbsp ground coriander
Salt and pepper to taste
⅔ cup sour cream
1 tsp rum

Melt the butter in a heavy saucepan and cook the onion until it is soft but not brown. Add the carrots, broth, coriander and salt and pepper to taste. Bring to the boil then simmer over a low heat for 25 minutes. Purée the mixture in a blender or food processor, then return it to the saucepan. Add the sour cream and rum. Heat the soup but do not let it boil.
Serves 4

Yellow Split Pea Soup

1 lb (450 g) smoked ham hocks
1 lb (450 g) dried yellow split peas, rinsed and picked over
3 slices fresh ginger, about the size of a small coin
2 cloves garlic, minced
12 cups water or stock
3 carrots, grated
1 large onion, chopped
2 tsp turmeric
1½ tsp chilli powder
Small piece fresh hot red pepper
1 tbsp rum
1½ tbsp chopped fresh coriander

Combine the first five ingredients in a saucepan, bring to the boil and simmer gently for 1 hour. Stir in the carrot, onion, turmeric, chilli powder and hot pepper, and simmer for a further 30 minutes. Remove the ham hocks and cut the meat from the bones. Return the meat to the soup, add the rum and coriander and simmer for a further 30 minutes. Discard the ginger and serve.
Serves 6

POULTRY

Pineapple Chicken with Yellow Rice

Olive Duck Casserole *(left)*, Duck with Rum Curry Glaze *(centre)* and Olive Chicken Casserole *(right)*

Turkey Breast with Rum Curry Glaze

1 3 – 4 lb (1 ½ – 2 kg) turkey breast,
  rolled and boned
Salt and pepper to taste

Glaze:
¼ cup honey
2 tbsp brown sugar
2 tbsp butter
2 tsp curry powder
1 tsp mustard (prepared)
2 tbsp rum

Preheat the oven to 350°F.

Season the turkey breast with salt and pepper. Tie it with string, if necessary, into a neat roll. Bake for 1 hour. Meanwhile, mix together the glaze ingredients in a heavy saucepan and heat until the sugar dissolves. Increase the oven temperature to 400°F. Brush the turkey with the glaze and bake for a further 30 – 40 minutes or until the turkey is brown, crisp and cooked through.
Serves 6 – 8

20

Alternatives

Stuffed Turkey Breast

Open the turkey breast, flatten it slightly with a meat mallet, stuff with 1 quantity of **Barbados Rum Fruit Stuffing** (recipe on page 56). Re-roll the breast, tie securely and bake as above.

Duck with Rum Curry Glaze

Use a duck instead of a turkey breast and proceed as above.

Rolled Pork Loin with Rum Curry Glaze

Use rolled pork loin in place of turkey breast and proceed as above.

Olive Duck Casserole

2 ducks, jointed
2 tbsp oil
2 tbsp brown sugar
2 cups stock or water
½ cup pimento stuffed olives

Marinade:
1 tsp salt
½ tsp pepper
3 onions, sliced thinly
4 blades chives, chopped
2 celery stalks, chopped
1 tsp dried thyme
1 tsp marjoram
1 tbsp Angostura bitters
4 tbsp Worcestershire sauce
2 cloves garlic, minced
¼ cup rum

Place the duck in a large bowl. Mix together all the marinade ingredients, pour over the duck, marinate overnight in the refrigerator.

Heat the oil in a heavy saucepan, add the sugar and cook until dark brown, about 3 – 4 minutes. *Do not overcook or the mixture will be bitter.* Scrape the seasoning from the duck. Cook the duck in the sugar and oil until deep brown. Add the reserved marinade, bring to the boil and boil for 5 minutes. Add the stock, cover, bring to the boil again. Reduce the heat and simmer for 40 minutes. Add the olives and simmer for a further 15 – 20 minutes or until the duck is tender.
Serves 6 – 8

Alternative
Olive Chicken Casserole

Cook as above but use chickens instead of ducks. Cook for a total of 45 minutes.

Paprika Duck

1 4 – 5 lb (2 – 2½ kg) duck, jointed
3 tbsp oil
4 tbsp paprika, divided 3 tbsp, 1 tbsp
Salt and pepper to taste
1 large onion, chopped
1 clove garlic, minced
2 tbsp flour
2½ cups chicken stock
4 tbsp rum
1 tomato, chopped
1 green sweet pepper, chopped
2 tsp finely minced parsley

Blend the oil and 3 tablespoons of paprika in a large saucepan. Season the duck pieces with salt and pepper and fry in the paprika mixture until brown all over. Remove the duck from the oil and fry the onion and garlic for 3 minutes. Stir in the flour then add the stock in a slow, steady stream, stirring all the time. Add the rum and cook, stirring, for a further 2 minutes. Add the duck, tomato and sweet pepper. Cover tightly and cook over a very low heat for 1 – 1½ hours or until the duck is tender. Sprinkle with the remaining 1 tablespoon of paprika and the parsley just before serving.
Serves 4 – 6

Alternative
Paprika Chicken

Cook as above but use a chicken instead of the duck. Cook the chicken for 40 – 45 minutes.

Fried Spiced Chicken

1 chicken, jointed
½ tsp salt
1 tsp Chinese five spice powder
¼ tsp black pepper
4 tbsp rum
Flour to coat chicken

Mix the salt, Chinese spice, pepper and rum together. Coat the chicken with the mixture and leave to marinate for 4 hours at room temperature.

Coat the chicken with the flour, half fill a deep frying pan with oil and deep fry the chicken until golden brown, about 30 minutes. Drain the chicken on a paper towel and sprinkle lightly with additional salt and pepper.
Serves 4

SDQ Chicken à la Judsy

1 chicken, cut into 2" (5 cm) pieces
3 limes
½ cup rum
¼ cup soy sauce
2 cloves garlic, minced
2 large onions, chopped finely
Salt and pepper to taste
Flour to coat

Place the chicken in a large bowl. Mix together the juice from the limes, the rum, the soy sauce, garlic, onions and salt and pepper to taste, and pour over the chicken. Marinate the chicken pieces in the mixture for 4 hours or longer. Drain the chicken, dip in flour to coat and deep fry for 10 minutes or until golden. Serve with additional lime wedges.
Serves 4

Roast Goose

1 goose
3 tbsp butter
1 onion, chopped
½ cup sliced mushrooms
½ cup pork sausage meat
1 cup breadcrumbs
1 cup chopped chestnuts or breadnuts
1 tbsp chopped parsley
4 tbsp Cockspur golden rum, divided
  2 tbsp, 2 tbsp
Salt and pepper to taste
6 rashers bacon
3 oranges, cut into segments

Preheat the oven to 400°F.

Melt the butter in a frying pan, sauté the onion and mushrooms for 5 minutes. Add the sausage meat, brown for 2 minutes. Stir in the breadcrumbs, nuts, parsley, 2 tablespoons of rum and salt and pepper to taste. Leave to cool to room temperature.

Stuff the goose with the cooled stuffing, lightly salt and pepper the outside of the goose. Place the bacon over the breast of the goose and place it on a rack in a baking pan containing ½ cup of water. Roast the goose in the oven for 30 minutes. Reduce the heat to 350°F and continue to cook, allowing a total of 20 minutes per pound (450 g), basting frequently with the pan juices. Remove to a serving dish, pour an additional 2 tablespoons of rum over the goose and ignite. Garnish with the orange segments.
Serves 8 – 10 depending on size of goose

Sticky Chicken *(left)*, Fried Spiced Chicken *(centre)* and Rum-Curried Chicken Crepes *(right)*

Pineapple Chicken with Yellow Rice

1 chicken, jointed
4 tbsp lime juice
Salt and pepper to taste
4 tbsp oil
¼ cup raisins
2 tbsp rum
Dash tabasco hot pepper sauce
2 tomatoes, diced coarsely
½ pineapple, cut into cubes
2 tbsp butter
1 tsp sugar

Rub the chicken with the lime juice and leave for 1 hour.

Season the chicken with salt and pepper, then fry in the oil until browned. Reduce the heat, cover the pan with a tight-fitting lid and cook for 10 minutes. Add the raisins, rum, tabasco and tomatoes. Cover, bring to the boil, reduce the heat and simmer for 20 – 25 minutes.

Meanwhile, as the chicken is cooking, fry the pineapple in the butter and sugar until golden brown, set aside and prepare the **Yellow Rice** (recipe on page 24).

23

Yellow Rice

1 onion, chopped
3 tbsp butter
1 ¼ cups rice
1 tsp turmeric powder
½ tsp salt
2 ½ cups chicken broth

Fry the onion in the butter for 2 minutes, add the rice and turmeric and fry until the rice is golden, about 2 minutes. Add the salt and broth. Cover tightly, bring to the boil, *immediately* reduce the heat to low and simmer for 20 minutes or until the rice is cooked thoroughly and the liquid evaporates.

To serve:
Place the rice in a ring mould, packing it in tightly. Turn out on a serving dish, put the chicken in the centre and garnish with the pineapple.
Serves 4 – 6

Tangy Grilled Chicken

Tangy Grilled Chicken

3 small chickens, halved
Salt and pepper to taste

Marinade:
2 large onions
4 cloves garlic
1 ½ cups ketchup
¾ cup water
½ cup oil
6 tbsp honey
3 tbsp rum
3 tbsp prepared mustard
1 ½ tbsp dried tarragon leaves

Sauce:
½ cup cream
Reserved marinade
¼ lb (225 g) butter, cut into pieces

Make the marinade. Chop the onions and garlic in a blender or food processor, add the remaining marinade ingredients and process for 10 seconds. Refrigerate 1 cup of marinade for the sauce. Season the chicken halves with salt and pepper and pour the remainder of the marinade over the chicken. Marinate for 8 hours or overnight in the refrigerator, turning several times.

Preheat the oven to 400°F.

Line a baking pan with foil, drain the chicken, reserving the marinade. Place the chicken on the foil, skin side up, and bake for 40 minutes, basting frequently.

Prepare the sauce. Boil the reserved refrigerated marinade with the cream until the sauce is reduced by half, about 10 minutes. Remove from the heat and whisk in the butter, a few pieces at a time.

Preheat the grill or broiler. Broil the chicken, skin side up, until brown. Reheat the sauce, pour some over the chicken and serve the remainder separately.
Serves 6

Fettuccine and Chicken *(top, left)* and Orange Chicken

Fettuccine and Chicken

4 chicken breasts, boned, skinned and
    cut into ¾" (2 cm) strips
All purpose flour
Salt and pepper to taste
¼ cup butter
3 sweet peppers, cut into julienne strips
2 large onions, sliced thinly
2 tbsp lime juice
1 tbsp grated lime peel
1 2" (5 cm) piece fresh ginger, minced
3 cloves garlic, minced
¼ tsp dried red pepper flakes
¼ cup rum
1 lb (450 g) fettuccine

Coriander (cilantro) butter:
½ cup butter, at room temperature
¼ cup fresh coriander (cilantro)
4 chives

Make the coriander butter. Place all the ingredients in a blender or food processor, blend until smooth.

Prepare the chicken. Season the flour with the salt and pepper. Dredge the chicken strips in the seasoned flour and brown, in the butter, on one side, for 3 minutes. Turn the chicken, add the peppers, onions, lime juice and peel, ginger, garlic and pepper flakes. Stir fry until the chicken is cooked, about 3 – 4 minutes. Pour the rum into a small pan and heat briefly. Ignite. Reduce the heat to low, add coriander (cilantro) butter by the spoonful and stir until incorporated. Add to the chicken and stir in.

Meanwhile, cook the fettuccine in a large pan of boiling, salted water until it is firm and cooked. Drain, place in a serving dish, pour the chicken over it, toss lightly and serve immediately.
Serves 6

25

Ali's Chicken

1 chicken, cut into pieces
2 tbsp oil
3 cloves garlic, minced
3 tbsp fresh ginger, minced
1 tbsp oyster sauce
⅓ cup soy sauce
1 tbsp brown sugar
⅛ cup rum
⅓ cup water

Heat the oil in a saucepan, fry the garlic and ginger for 2 minutes. Add the chicken and brown it. Add the remaining ingredients. Cover the pan, bring to the boil and reduce the heat. Simmer for 40 – 45 minutes or until the chicken is tender.
Serves 4 – 6

Fruited Chicken

2 chicken breast halves, boned and
  skinned
¼ cup flour
Salt and pepper to taste
1 egg, beaten
2 tbsp olive oil
2 bananas, sliced thickly
½ cup pineapple wedges
½ tsp freshly grated nutmeg
½ tsp cinnamon
Dash allspice
¼ cup rum
¼ cup cream
2 tbsp toasted unsweetened coconut
  flakes
2 tsp grated orange peel

Season the flour with salt and pepper, dip the chicken in the egg then the flour mixture and fry in the olive oil for 3 – 4 minutes per side

or until cooked. Transfer the chicken to a serving dish and keep it warm.

Add the bananas, pineapple, nutmeg, cinnamon and allspice to the oil in the pan, cook for 5 minutes, then pour in the rum. Heat briefly and ignite. When the flames subside, add the cream and simmer until thick, about 2 minutes. Stir any accumulated juices from the chicken into the sauce in the pan. Pour the sauce over the chicken. Sprinkle with the coconut and orange peel.
Serves 2

Sticky Chicken

1 chicken, cut into pieces
½ cup vinegar
½ cup sugar
½ cup soy sauce
3 cloves garlic, minced
2 tbsp freshly grated ginger
¼ cup Cockspur golden rum

Put the chicken in a bowl. Mix together the rest of the ingredients and pour over the chicken. Leave the chicken to marinate in the refrigerator for 8 hours or overnight, turning frequently to coat with marinade.

Place all the ingredients in a heavy saucepan and bring to the boil. Cover tightly, reduce the heat and simmer for 15 minutes. Uncover the pan and simmer for a further 20 minutes. Remove the chicken from the pan and keep it warm. Continue simmering the sauce until it caramelises, about 10 – 15 minutes. Pour the sauce over the chicken.
Serves 4 – 6

Curried Chicken

Rum Punch Chicken

3 lb (1 ½ kg) chicken pieces
2 tbsp oil
1 tsp salt
⅛ tsp black pepper
¾ cup light corn syrup
½ cup rum
Dash tabasco hot pepper sauce
¼ cup lime juice
1 tbsp cornstarch
1 – 2 tsp grated lime peel

Heat the oil in a large, heavy saucepan and fry the chicken until golden brown. Sprinkle with salt and pepper. Mix together the corn syrup, the rum, the tabasco and the lime juice. Spoon 3 tablespoons of the mixture over the chicken. Cover and cook over a low heat for 40 minutes. Remove the chicken to a serving dish and keep it warm.

Add the cornstarch to the remainder of the syrup mixture and stir it into the pan, stirring constantly until the sauce is thick, about 6 minutes. Spoon the sauce over the chicken and garnish with the grated lime peel.
Serves 4 – 6

Curried Chicken

1 chicken, cut into pieces
2 large onions, chopped
3 cloves garlic, minced
1 ½ tbsp curry powder
1 tbsp Worcestershire sauce
1 tbsp rum
2 tsp cumin seed (jeera), divided
Salt and pepper to taste
1 tbsp oil
½ cup chicken stock or water

In a large bowl mix together the onions, garlic, curry powder, Worcestershire sauce, rum, 1 teaspoon of the cumin, and salt and pepper to taste. Add the chicken, mix well and marinate for 4 hours.

In a heavy saucepan, brown the rest of the cumin in the oil until fragrant, drain the chicken and brown in the oil until golden. Add the marinade and the stock or water. Bring to the boil, cover tightly, reduce heat and simmer for 45 minutes.
Serves 4 – 6

Rum-Curried Chicken Crepes

½ cup chopped onion
½ cup chopped celery
¼ cup butter
1 tbsp curry powder
¼ cup flour
1 cup milk
1 ½ cups chicken stock
½ tsp salt
Dash black pepper
1 tbsp rum
3 cups cooked chopped chicken
10 cooked crepes
⅓ cup grated Parmesan cheese

Preheat the oven to 350°F.

Fry the onion and celery in the butter for 3 minutes. Add the curry powder and fry for 1 minute. Add the flour, stir until it is mixed in. Slowly add the milk, stirring all the time, then similarly add the stock. Cook, stirring, until thick. Remove from the heat, add the salt, pepper and rum. Mix 1 cup of the sauce into the chicken. Spoon 3 tablespoons of the chicken mixture onto each crepe, roll them up and place them in a greased baking dish. Pour the remainder of the sauce over the crepes. Sprinkle with the Parmesan cheese and bake in the oven for 20 – 25 minutes.
Serves 4 – 5

Orange Chicken

1 chicken, cut into pieces
Salt and pepper to taste
2 tsp curry powder
¼ cup orange juice
Grated rind of one orange
2 tbsp honey
1 tbsp prepared mustard
1 tbsp rum
2 tsp cornstarch
4 tbsp water
½ orange, peeled and sliced for garnish

Preheat the oven to 375°F.

Mix the salt and pepper with the curry powder and rub into the chicken pieces. Place the chicken pieces in a baking pan, skin sides down. Mix together the orange juice, rind, honey, mustard and rum. Pour over the chicken and bake in the oven for 30 minutes. Turn the chicken skin sides up, baste with the pan juices and cook for a further 20 – 30 minutes or until done. Remove the chicken to a serving dish. Mix the cornstarch and water, add to the pan juices and stir over a low heat, incorporating any browned bits in the pan. Cook until the sauce is slightly thickened. Pour over the chicken and garnish with orange slices.
Serves 4 – 6

Hawaiian Chicken

2 chickens, cut into pieces
¼ cup melted butter
Salt and pepper to taste
1 tin pineapple slices, drained (reserve
* juice for sauce)*

Sauce:
½ cup melted butter
1 tsp cornstarch
1 tsp grated lime or lemon peel
¼ cup lime or lemon juice
⅓ cup pineapple syrup (reserved)
2 tbsp grated onion
2 tsp soy sauce
½ tsp dry thyme
1 tbsp rum

In a medium saucepan, combine the sauce ingredients. Cook until the sauce is slightly thickened. Set aside.

Preheat the grill or broiler. Place the chicken on the broiler rack, brush with half of the melted butter and broil for 15 minutes. Sprinkle the chicken lightly with salt and pepper and turn it over. Brush with the remaining butter and broil for a further 15 minutes. Sprinkle the chicken lightly with salt and pepper. Brush with the sauce mixture and broil for 5 minutes, turn, brush again with the sauce, adding pineapple slices dipped in the sauce to the broiler pan, and broil again for a further 5 – 10 minutes or until the chicken is glazed and cooked. Serve remaining sauce separately.
Serves 6 – 8

Caribbean Chicken Legs

4 chicken drumsticks
4 chicken thighs
¼ cup rum
1 tbsp chilli powder
1 tbsp molasses
¼ tsp tabasco hot pepper sauce
Salt and pepper to taste

Grilled pineapple:
1 pineapple
¼ cup honey

Prepare the chicken. Mix the rum, chilli powder, molasses, tabasco and salt and pepper together, pour over the chicken and leave to marinate for at least 2 hours or overnight in the refrigerator.

Remove the chicken from the marinade and grill it for 15 – 20 minutes. Turn the chicken over and grill for a further 15 – 20 minutes.

Prepare the grilled pineapple. Cut the pineapple into 8 wedges, leaving on the rind. Dribble the honey over it and let it stand for 1 hour. Grill, rind side down, for 15 minutes.

Serve the chicken garnished with the grilled pineapple.
Serves 4

Barbados Party Chicken Pelao

2 chickens, cut into joints
1 tomato, diced
1 sweet pepper, diced
1 tsp dried thyme
½ tsp marjoram
3 tbsp Worcestershire sauce
1 large piece hot red pepper
2 large onions, diced
2 cloves garlic, minced
1 tsp salt
½ tsp pepper
½ cup Cockspur golden rum
1 tbsp Angostura bitters
2 tbsp oil
¼ cup brown sugar
2 cups rice
3¾ cups water or chicken stock
1 tin pigeon peas, drained
½ cup raisins
½ cup pimento stuffed olives

Place the chicken in a large bowl. Mix together the tomato, sweet pepper, thyme, marjoram, Worcestershire sauce, hot pepper, onions, garlic, salt, pepper, rum and Angostura bitters. Toss well to combine ingredients and pour over the chicken. Leave to marinate overnight in the refrigerator.

In a large, heavy saucepan, heat the oil and sugar until the sugar is very dark, about 4 – 5 minutes on high. *Do not let it burn.*

Drain the chicken, reserving the marinade, and brown it all over, in batches, in the sugar and oil. Return all the chicken and the marinade to the saucepan, cover tightly and bring to the boil. Lower the heat and simmer for 15 minutes. Add the rice and water or stock, cover, bring to the boil, reduce the heat and cook for a further 10 minutes. Add the pigeon peas, raisins and olives, cover and continue to simmer until the rice is cooked thoroughly and the liquid has evaporated, about 15 – 20 minutes more.

This is excellent to serve on picnics. Just wrap the saucepan in several layers of newspaper. It keeps warm for hours!
Serves 8 – 10

Simple Pelao

Marinate the chicken as above for a few hours at room temperature, cook as above, omitting the peas, raisins and olives.

Oriental Hoisin Chicken

1 chicken, cut into pieces
Salt and pepper to taste
¼ cup hoisin sauce
2 tbsp rum
2 tbsp soy sauce
1 clove garlic, minced
1 tsp powdered ginger
¼ tsp tabasco hot pepper sauce

Season the chicken with salt and pepper. Mix the rest of the ingredients together and set aside.

Grill the chicken over medium coals for 20 – 25 minutes, turning often to ensure that it does not burn. Baste the chicken with the hoisin sauce mixture. Continue cooking and basting for a further 20 – 25 minutes or until the chicken is cooked.
Serves 4 – 6

Barbados Party Chicken Pelao

BEEF AND LAMB

Lamb Kebabs

Marinated Barbecue Steaks

4 rib eye or cube steaks

Marinade:
2 tbsp vinegar
2 tbsp olive oil
2 tbsp rum
2 tbsp sugar
1 tsp salt
¼ tsp black pepper
1 tsp dried rosemary
1 onion, chopped finely
1 clove garlic, minced
2 tbsp soy sauce

Blend all the marinade ingredients in a shallow dish. Add the steaks, turning them to coat them well. Leave to marinate for two to three hours.

Barbecue the steaks over hot coals, basting frequently, until they are ready.
Serves 4

Marinated Barbecue Steak

Beef Kidneys

2 lb (1 kg) beef kidneys, sliced thinly
Salt and pepper to taste
1 tbsp rum
½ tsp dried thyme
6 tbsp butter
1 large onion, sliced thinly
¼ cup dry sherry
1 tsp cornstarch

Mix together the salt, pepper, rum and thyme and marinate the kidneys in this mixture for 30 minutes.

Heat 3 tablespoons butter in a heavy saucepan, add the kidneys, and stir fry for 5 – 10 minutes or until the kidneys are cooked through. Remove the kidneys from the saucepan. Heat the remaining 3 table-spoons butter in the saucepan, fry the onions until they are golden and soft. Dissolve the cornstarch in the sherry, add to the onion mixture in the saucepan and stir until thickened. Add the kidneys and cook until heated through.
Serves 4

Beef Kidneys

Oxtail Stew

3 – 4 lb (1 ½ – 2 kg) oxtail, cut into pieces
2 tbsp oil
3 carrots, sliced
3 onions, sliced
3 cloves garlic, minced
½ tsp dried thyme
1 tsp curry powder
1 16 oz (450 g) tin tomatoes, chopped,
  with liquid
1 tbsp Worcestershire sauce
Salt and pepper to taste
4 tbsp Cockspur golden rum

Fry the carrots, onions, garlic, thyme and curry powder in the oil until the onions are soft. Add the oxtail and brown lightly. Add the chopped tomatoes with the liquid, the Worcestershire sauce, salt, pepper and rum. Cover, bring to the boil, reduce the heat and simmer for 2 hours or until the meat is tender. Remove the cover, check the seasoning and boil vigorously until the stew thickens slightly.
Serves 4 – 6

Lamb Kebabs

2 lb (1 kg) lamb, cut into 1 ½" (3 ½ cm)
  cubes
1 onion, minced
½ tsp salt
2 cloves garlic, minced
¼ cup red wine
¼ cup corn oil or olive oil
2 tbsp oregano
1 tsp crushed rosemary
2 tbsp rum
Dash black pepper
Green pepper wedges
Tomato wedges
Onion wedges

Combine the minced onion, salt, garlic, wine, oil, oregano, rosemary, rum and pepper. Pour the mixture over the lamb cubes and marinate overnight in the refrigerator.

Thread onto skewers, alternating the lamb with wedges of green pepper, tomato and onion. Grill for 10 minutes each side.
Serves 4

West Indian Beef Stew

2 lb (1 kg) stewing steak, cut ¾ – 1"
    (2 – 2½ cm) thick
1 tsp salt
¼ tsp black pepper
1 tsp dried thyme
½ tsp dried marjoram
4 blades chives, chopped
2 large onions, chopped
2 cloves garlic, minced
Small piece hot red pepper, chopped
4 tbsp rum
3 tbsp Worcestershire sauce
3 tbsp oil
3 tbsp brown sugar
1 carrot, sliced
2 cups water or beef broth
3 potatoes, quartered

Place the beef in a large bowl. Mix together the salt, pepper, thyme, marjoram, chives, onions, garlic, hot pepper, rum and Worcestershire sauce. Pour over the beef and leave to marinate for at least 1 hour. Heat the oil in a heavy saucepan, add the sugar and brown for 3 minutes. Drain the meat, reserving the marinade, and brown it in the oil and sugar. Add the marinade and fry for 3 minutes. Add the carrot and the stock. Bring to the boil, lower the heat and simmer gently for 1 hour. Add the potatoes and additional liquid if required. Cook until the potatoes are tender and the gravy has thickened.
Serves 4 – 6

Rum Chilli

1 lb (450 g) minced beef
2 tbsp oil
1 large onion, sliced
2 cloves garlic, minced
1 large sweet pepper, cut into strips
2 tbsp chilli powder
¼ tsp dried chilli flakes
½ tsp ground cumin
½ tsp oregano
Salt and pepper to taste
1 16 oz (450 g) tin tomatoes with liquid
1 16 oz (450 g) tin tomato sauce
1 16 oz (450 g) tin kidney beans
3 tbsp rum

Heat the oil in a frying pan. Fry the meat in the oil until browned. Add the onion, garlic, sweet pepper, chilli powder, chilli flakes, cumin and oregano. Fry for 3 minutes. Add the tomatoes, breaking them into pieces, and the tomato sauce. Season with salt and pepper to taste. Lower the heat and simmer for at least 1 hour, adding more liquid if necessary. Add the beans and simmer for 30 minutes more. Add the rum just before serving.
Serves 4

Olive Beef Casserole

2 lb (1 kg) stewing beef
½ cup flour
1 tsp salt
¼ tsp black pepper
4 tbsp oil
4 onions, chopped coarsely
2 large sweet peppers, chopped coarsely
4 cloves garlic, minced
3 tbsp tomato paste
2 tsp sugar
1 bay leaf
2 tsp tabasco hot pepper sauce
1 cup water
16 pimento stuffed olives
3 tomatoes, cut into wedges
2 tbsp rum

Combine the flour, salt and pepper. Toss the beef in the seasoned flour and brown the meat in the oil. Remove the meat from the pan, fry the onions and sweet peppers, over a moderate heat, for 5 minutes. Add the garlic and cook for 1 minute. Add the tomato paste, sugar, bay leaf, tabasco and water. Add the beef, cover, bring to the boil. Reduce the heat and simmer until the beef is tender (about 1 hour). Add the olives, tomatoes and rum, reheat for 2 minutes.
Serves 4 – 6

Mushroom Veal Cordon-Bleu

4 ready-breaded veal cordon bleu (defrosted)
2 tbsp butter
2 tbsp olive oil
2 tbsp rum
1 can mushroom soup
½ soup can of milk
Salt and pepper to taste

Melt the butter and oil in large frying pan. Cook the veal until it is crisp and done, about 5 minutes each side. Remove the veal from the pan and keep it warm. Pour the rum into the pan, ignite and, when the flames subside, add the soup and milk, stirring until the mixture is smooth. Add the salt and pepper to taste, pour the sauce over the veal.
Serves 4

PORK

Orange Sauced Pork Roast *(top, left)* with Orange Sauce *(bottom, left)*, Spareribs Caribbean *(right)* and Caribbean Pork Tenderloin *(centre)*

Spicy Orange Pork Kebabs

Hawaiian Pork Roast

3 ½ – 4 lb (2 kg) pork loin, boned and
*   rolled*
2 tsp salt
½ tsp pepper

Pineapple glaze:
1 9 oz (250 g) can crushed pineapple
1 cup brown sugar
3 tbsp lime juice
2 tbsp rum
2 tbsp prepared mustard

Preheat the oven to 375°F.

Season the loin roast with salt and pepper. Bake in the oven for 1 hour and 15 minutes. Increase the oven temperature to 425°F, baste the pork with some of the glaze and bake for a further 10 minutes. Baste again with some of the glaze and bake for a further 10 minutes or until cooked thoroughly. Serve the remaining glaze with the roast.

To make the glaze:
Combine all the ingredients in a medium saucepan. Cook over a medium heat, stirring until the sugar dissolves.
Serves 6 – 8

Spareribs Caribbean

3 lb (1 ½ kg) pork spareribs, left whole
Salt and pepper to taste
1 8 oz (250 g) tin tomato sauce
½ cup rum
1 cup honey
2 tbsp lime juice
1 medium onion, minced
4 large cloves garlic, minced
2 tbsp Worcestershire sauce
⅛ tsp cayenne pepper

Season the spareribs with salt and pepper, place them in a large baking pan. Mix the remaining ingredients together, pour the mixture over the ribs and leave to marinate for 8 hours or overnight in the refrigerator, turning frequently.

Preheat the oven to 350°F.

Bake the spareribs for about 1 hour, turning and basting frequently. Place the spareribs under the grill and grill for 5 minutes. Cut into individual ribs and serve.
Serves 4

40

Spicy Orange Pork Kebabs

2 lb (1 kg) boneless pork, cut into 1½"
  (3½ cm) cubes
¼ cup dark brown sugar
¼ cup red wine vinegar
¼ tsp dried hot pepper flakes
1½ tbsp freshly grated orange rind
1 tbsp Worcestershire sauce
1 tbsp rum
2 tbsp honey
¼ cup fresh orange juice
¼ cup butter
1 large sweet pepper, cut into large cubes
8 small onions, parboiled
1 large orange, cut into eighths
Salt and pepper to taste

In a small saucepan, combine the brown sugar, vinegar, pepper flakes, orange rind, Worcestershire sauce, rum, honey, orange juice and butter. Heat the mixture until the butter melts, stirring occasionally. Thread skewers with the pork, the pepper, the onion and the orange wedges. Season lightly with salt and pepper.

Grease a Swiss roll pan, put the skewers on it and grill, 4" (10 cm) from the heat, for 10 – 12 minutes each side or until the kebabs are cooked thoroughly. Alternatively, place kebabs over hot coals on the barbecue and cook for 12 – 14 minutes per side, basting and turning all the time.
Serves 4 – 6

Hawaiian Pork Roast (left) and Simple Spareribs (right)

Simple Spareribs

3 lb (1 ½ kg) lean pork spareribs (left in
  one piece)
2 tsp liquid smoke barbecue flavouring
2 tbsp rum
1 ½ tsp adobo (Latin seasoning available
  in supermarkets)
Black pepper to taste

Rub one side of the spareribs with 1 teaspoon
smoke, 1 tablespoon rum, ¾ teaspoon adobo
and pepper to taste, turn the spareribs over
and repeat the seasoning in the same way.
Place the spareribs on a piece of foil on a
preheated barbecue grill at high setting, close
the grill and cook for 15 minutes. Turn and
continue to cook for a further 10 – 15 minutes
or until the spareribs are cooked thoroughly.
Cut through bones to separate ribs and serve.
Serves 4

Rum Mustard Glazed Ham

1 3 lb (1 ½ kg) smoked ham, defrosted
¼ cup brown sugar
1 tbsp dry mustard
2 tbsp rum
Whole cloves and pineapple slices to
  garnish

Preheat the oven to 350°F.
    Mix together the brown sugar, mustard
and rum. Remove the skin from the ham,
score the fat and stud with cloves. Bake the
ham for 30 minutes. Pour half of the rum mixture over the ham and roast for a further 15
minutes. Place pineapple rings on the ham,
fasten them with toothpicks. Pour over the
remaining rum mixture and bake for a further
20 minutes or until cooked thoroughly.
Remove toothpicks and serve.
Serves 6 – 8

Buffet Ham Slices

1 5 lb (2 ½ kg) ham
⅓ cup frozen concentrated pineapple or
  orange juice
⅓ cup maple syrup
⅓ cup rum

Preheat the oven to 325°F.
    Remove the skin from the ham, score
the fat, wrap tightly in foil and bake for 30
minutes. Pour off all the liquid. Mix together
the fruit juice, syrup and rum. Pour the
mixture over the ham, cover loosely with the
foil and bake for 2 hours more. Cool the ham
for 20 minutes, slice neatly and serve.
Serves 12 – 14

Lime Spareribs

1 2 – 3 lb (1 – 1 ½ kg) rack of spareribs,
  left whole
Grated rind and juice of 2 limes
¼ tsp garlic powder
1 tsp ground ginger
2 tbsp brown sugar
2 tbsp rum
2 tbsp orange liqueur
2 tbsp soy sauce
Salt and pepper to taste

Mix together the rind and juice of the limes
with the garlic powder, ginger, sugar, rum,
orange liqueur and soy sauce. Pour over the
spareribs and leave to marinate for several
hours or overnight in the refrigerator.
    Season the spareribs lightly with salt and
pepper. Grill over hot coals for 15 minutes
each side, or until cooked thoroughly,
basting frequently with the marinade.
Serves 3 – 4

Stuffed Suckling Pig

1 suckling pig, about 20 lb (10 kg)
Vinegar
1 clove garlic, cut
Salt and pepper
Rum
Oil
1 red apple

Stuffing:
4 tbsp melted butter
2 large onions, chopped
1 clove garlic, minced
1 sweet pepper, chopped
1½ lb (750 g) fresh breadcrumbs
4 tbsp Cockspur golden rum
1 tbsp powdered ginger
1½ tsp salt
½ tsp black pepper
1 tsp dried thyme
½ tsp freshly grated nutmeg
½ cup raisins
2 tbsp Worcestershire sauce
1 egg, lightly beaten

Prepare the stuffing by heating the butter in a frying pan and frying the onions, garlic and sweet pepper for 5 minutes. Add the breadcrumbs, rum, ginger, salt, pepper, thyme and nutmeg. Cook, stirring, for 3 minutes, remove from heat and stir in the raisins, Worcestershire sauce and egg. Mix the stuffing thoroughly and allow it to cool completely.

Preheat the oven to 375°F.

Prepare the suckling pig by wiping it inside and out with a cloth wrung out in vinegar. Rub inside and out with the cut clove of garlic then sprinkle with salt and pepper to taste. Brush with rum inside and out. Stuff the cavity with the stuffing, sew together, prop open the mouth with a small wooden block. Tie to fit into the baking pan in a sitting position. Rub the outside again with the vinegared cloth, brush with oil again and roast in the oven for 4 – 5 hours or until cooked thoroughly, basting frequently with oil. Remove the wood from the mouth, stuff the mouth with the red apple.
Serves 10 – 14

Fried Pork Strips with Scallion Sauce

1½ lb (750 g) pork cut into ¾" (2 cm)
   strips
1 tsp rum
⅓ cup finely chopped onion
Salt to taste
Ground black pepper to taste
2 tsp finely minced fresh ginger
2 tbsp soy sauce
2½ tsp white vinegar
1 tsp honey
2 tsp brown sugar
½ tsp cornstarch
4 tbsp thinly sliced scallions
Flour for dredging
Vegetable oil for frying

In a bowl, mix together the pork, rum, onion, salt and pepper to taste. Marinate for 30 minutes.

In a small saucepan, mix together the ginger, soy sauce, vinegar, honey, sugar and cornstarch, stirring to dissolve the cornstarch. Bring to the boil, then stir until the sugar dissolves and the sauce is slightly thickened. Remove from the heat and stir in the scallions. Set aside.

Dredge the pork, with any onion adhering to it, in the flour. Deep fry the strips in oil, drain on paper towels and serve with the sauce.
Serves 4

Honeyed Pork Chops

4 pork chops
Salt and pepper to taste

Marinade:
¼ cup honey
¼ cup soy sauce
1 tbsp rum
2 tsp ground fresh ginger
1 tsp prepared mustard

Combine all the ingredients for the marinade. Pour it over the pork and leave to marinate for several hours or overnight in the refrigerator.

Grill or barbecue the pork until it is cooked thoroughly, turning and basting with marinade frequently. This will take about 15 minutes per side, depending on the thickness of the pork.
Serves 4

Rolled Pork Loin with Rum Curry Glaze

See the alternative to **Turkey Breast with Rum Curry Glaze** on page 20.

Pork Roast

3 lb (1 ½ kg) leg of pork roast
1 tbsp rum
Juice of 1 lime
1 clove garlic, sliced thin
1 tsp dried sage
Salt and pepper to taste

Preheat the oven to 375°F.

Score the skin of the pork in neat squares. Sprinkle the meat side *only* with the rum and half of the lime juice. Make small cuts in the meaty side of the pork and insert garlic slivers. Rub the sage, salt and pepper on the meat side *only*.

Place the pork in a roasting pan. Rub the skin with the remainder of the lime juice, rub generously with salt and bake in the oven for 1½ hours or until the meat is cooked thoroughly and the skin is crisp. If the skin does not crisp, remove it from the pork and place it under the grill for a few minutes. Slice and serve.
Serves 4 – 6

Honeyed Pork Chops

Pork Roast

Oriental Spareribs

2 lb (1 kg) spareribs, left whole
3 tbsp orange flavoured liqueur
1 tsp grated orange rind
3 tbsp soy sauce
1 tsp ground ginger
1 clove garlic, minced
1 tbsp rum
Salt and pepper to taste

Mix together the liqueur, orange rind, soy sauce, ginger, garlic and rum. Pour over the spareribs and leave to marinate for at least 4 hours.

Remove the spareribs from the marinade, season with salt and pepper. Grill over hot coals for 15 minutes each side, or until the meat is thoroughly cooked, basting frequently.
Serves 4

Molasses Rum Glazed Pork

1 lb (450 g) pork tenderloin
3 tbsp butter
Salt and pepper to taste
½ tsp dried thyme
2 tbsp molasses
1 tbsp rum

Preheat the oven to 425°F.

Melt the butter in a saucepan large enough to hold the tenderloin. Season the pork with salt, pepper and thyme and fry it in the butter until brown. Remove the pork and set aside. To the same pan add the molasses and rum, heat gently. Coat the tenderloin with the rum and molasses mixture and bake for 25 – 30 minutes or until thoroughly cooked, turning occasionally. Slice thinly and serve.
Serves 2

Orange Sauced Pork Roast

4 lb (2 kg) pork loin, boned and rolled
Salt and pepper to taste

Orange sauce:
1 tbsp flour
5 tbsp water
2 tbsp fat from roast
1 tbsp butter
Salt and pepper to taste
Pinch cayenne pepper
⅔ cup fresh orange juice
4 tsp grated orange rind
1 tbsp guava or redcurrant jelly
1 tbsp rum

Preheat the oven to 375°F.

Season the pork loin with salt and pepper and bake for 1 hour and 10 minutes. Glaze with ¼ cup of the orange sauce and bake a further 20 minutes or until cooked through.

Sauce:
To make the sauce, mix the flour and water to a smooth paste, add the butter and the fat from the pan, stirring all the time. Season with salt, pepper and cayenne, add the orange juice and most of the rind. Simmer over a low heat, stirring constantly, for 5 – 8 minutes. Add the redcurrant jelly and the rum, cook until the jelly *just* melts.

Serve sprinkled with the remaining rind and garnish with orange slices if desired.
Serves 6 – 8

Caribbean Pork Tenderloin

1½ lb (750 g) piece of pork tenderloin
  cut into 6 steaks
Salt and pepper to taste
1 tbsp oil
¼ cup brown sugar
½ tsp freshly grated nutmeg
¼ tsp ground allspice
¼ tsp cinnamon
¼ tsp black pepper
⅓ cup fresh lime juice
¼ cup rum
4 oz (125 g) butter cut into pieces

Season the tenderloin steaks with salt and pepper. Heat the oil in a frying pan and fry the steaks in the oil until they are done, about 10 minutes. Remove from the pan and keep them warm. Deglaze the pan with 2 tablespoons water, scraping up the brown bits. Add the sugar, nutmeg, allspice, cinnamon, black pepper and lime juice. Cook for 2 minutes. Add the rum, ignite, reduce the heat to low and add the butter, one piece at a time, whisking in the next piece of butter just before the last melts. Spoon the sauce over the pork and serve.
Serves 2 – 3

FISH

Barbecued Fish with Rum-Ginger Sauce *(left)* and Shrimp Kebabs *(right)*

Marinated Barbecued Fish Steaks

4 lb (2 kg) fish steaks, cut 1" (2½ cm)
  thick
2 tbsp lime juice
2 tbsp olive oil
2 tbsp rum
1½ tsp salt
1 tsp sugar
1 onion, chopped
1 clove garlic, minced
¼ piece small red hot pepper, chopped
  finely
1 tsp thyme

Mix together the lime juice, olive oil, rum, salt, sugar, onion, garlic, hot pepper and thyme. Marinate the fish steaks in this mixture for 10 minutes on each side. Grease a hamburger grill, place the fish on the rack and barbecue for 6 minutes each side, or until cooked, turning once and brushing with a little marinade. *Do not overcook,* fish should be timed carefully and checked frequently.
Serves 8

Orange Gingered Fish

2 lb (1 kg) fish steaks, cut 1" (2½ cm)
  thick
Salt and pepper to taste

Marinade:
1 tsp finely grated orange rind
⅓ cup fresh orange juice
2 tbsp oil
2 tbsp soy sauce
1 tbsp cider vinegar
1 tbsp sugar
2 tsp finely grated fresh ginger
1 tbsp rum

Combine all the ingredients for the marinade. Season the fish with salt and pepper to taste. Pour the marinade over the fish and leave to marinate for 30 – 45 minutes.

Oil a hamburger grill basket, place the fish on it and barbecue the fish steaks for 6 minutes each side, basting frequently with the marinade.
Serves 4

Barbecued Fish with Rum-Ginger Sauce

2 lb (1 kg) firm white fish, cut into 1"
  (2½ cm) steaks
Salt and pepper to taste

Rum-Ginger sauce:
½ cup butter
1 tbsp lime juice
1 tbsp minced fresh ginger
1 tbsp rum

Make the rum-ginger sauce by combining all the ingredients in a saucepan and cooking until the butter *just barely* melts.

Lightly salt and pepper the fish steaks. Oil a hamburger grill basket, place the fish on it and barbecue the fish steaks over hot coals for 10 – 15 minutes or until they are thoroughly cooked, turning frequently and basting with the rum-ginger sauce. Serve the remaining sauce in a sauceboat.
Serves 4

Battered Fried Fish

Battered Fried Fish

1 lb (450 g) fish steaks
1 cup flour
½ tsp salt
½ tsp baking powder
1 egg
1 cup milk
1 tbsp rum
Salt and pepper
Ground ginger
¼ cup additional flour
Oil for frying

Mix 1 cup flour with the ½ teaspoon salt, baking powder, egg, milk and rum. Sprinkle the fish lightly with salt, pepper and ground ginger. Coat completely in the ¼ cup of flour, dip in the batter and deep fry until golden and cooked.
Serves 2 – 3

Mustard Sauced Fish

2 lb (1 kg) fish steaks
2 tsp rum (separated)
Ground ginger
Salt and pepper
Butter for greasing
½ cup mayonnaise
1 ½ tsp prepared mustard
1 small onion, chopped finely
Paprika

Sprinkle 1 teaspoon rum over the fish, then sprinkle with ginger, salt and pepper. Place in a buttered baking dish and leave for 10 minutes.

Preheat the oven to 425°F.

Mix together the mayonnaise, the second teaspoon rum, the mustard and the onion. Place the mixture in mounds over the fish. Sprinkle with paprika and bake for 20 – 25 minutes.
Serves 4

49

Shrimp Kebabs

2 lb (1 kg) shelled and deveined shrimps
1 16 oz (450 g) tin pineapple chunks,
   drained (reserve juice)
2 tbsp soy sauce
1 tbsp rum
1 tsp sugar
1 tsp ground ginger
Salt and pepper to taste
1 sweet pepper, cut into chunks

Mix together the soy sauce, rum, sugar, ginger, salt and pepper and juice from the pineapple. Pour the mixture over the shrimps and chill for at least 1 hour.

Thread shrimps, sweet pepper and pineapple on to skewers. Grill or barbecue for 5 minutes, turning and basting frequently. Continue cooking, checking the kebabs carefully, for a further 3 – 4 minutes or until they are cooked thoroughly.
Serves 6

Pepper Broiled Fish

6 6 oz (180 g) fish steaks
1 cup dry white breadcrumbs
½ cup butter, at room temperature
¼ cup minced chives
2 tbsp szechuan peppercorns
2 tbsp black peppercorns
2 tsp minced garlic
1 tsp ground ginger
Salt to taste

Sauce:
2 cups sour cream
⅛ cup rum
5 tbsp lime juice
3 tbsp green peppercorns
2 tbsp sugar

Mix the breadcrumbs, butter, chives, szechuan and black peppercorns and garlic in a blender or food processor and mix until the peppercorns are coarsely ground. Sprinkle the fish with salt and ginger. Brush the fish liberally with the butter and crumb mixture.

Preheat a broiler pan, grease the rack and broil the fish on high for 7 minutes. *Do not overcook.* Turn the fish, brush again liberally with the butter and crumb mixture and broil for a further 1 – 2 minutes or until it is crusty and cooked through. Serve immediately with the sauce.

To make the sauce, combine all the ingredients thoroughly.
Serves 6

Dad's Banana-Rum Fish

2 lb (1 kg) fish steaks
2 bananas, mashed
¼ cup condensed milk
½ cup mayonnaise
Salt and pepper to taste
Ground ginger
2 tbsp rum
Grated coconut

Preheat the oven to 400°F.

Mix together the bananas, condensed milk and mayonnaise. Place the fish in a well-oiled baking dish. Sprinkle with salt, pepper and ginger. Cover with the banana mixture, sprinkle with rum, then more ginger, then coconut. Bake for 15 – 20 minutes.
Serves 4

Rum Fried Fish *(left)*, Curried Shrimp Crêpes *(centre)* and Stewed Fish *(right)*

Rum Fried Fish

2 lb (1 kg) fish steaks
  or 10 flying fish
Ground ginger
Bajan seasoning if desired
½ cup flour
¼ tsp baking powder
Salt and pepper to taste
1 tbsp milk
2 eggs
1 tbsp rum
1 cup fresh breadcrumbs
Oil for frying

Bajan seasoning:
1 chopped chive
1 tsp lime juice
Salt and pepper to taste
1 piece hot red pepper
Pinch dried thyme
Pinch marjoram
Dash Worcestershire sauce

Prepare the Bajan seasoning. Combine the chopped chive, lime juice, salt, pepper, hot red pepper, a pinch each of dried thyme and marjoram and a dash of Worcestershire sauce thoroughly together.

Sprinkle the fish with the ground ginger. Stuff with Bajan seasoning if desired. (For fish steaks, cut gashes at regular intervals and stuff, for flying fish stuff between natural ridges.)

Mix the flour, baking powder, salt and pepper, and set aside. Mix the milk, eggs and rum, and set aside.

Coat the fish in the flour mixture, then the egg mixture then the breadcrumbs, ensuring that the fish is completely coated each time.

Place the prepared fish on a cake-cooling rack and refrigerate for at least 30 minutes to allow the coating to become firm.

Fry the fish in about ½″ (1 cm) of oil until crisp (about 2 minutes per side).
Serves 5

Curried Shrimp Crêpes

1 lb (450 g) cooked shrimps (reserve a
  few for garnishing)
¼ cup butter
½ cup finely chopped onions
½ cup finely chopped celery
1 clove garlic, minced
¼ cup finely chopped green pepper
1 tbsp curry powder
¼ cup flour
2½ cups milk
1 tsp lime juice
½ tsp salt
½ tsp ground ginger
1 tbsp rum
10 – 12 cooked crepes
Mango chutney to serve

Preheat the oven to 375°F.

Melt the butter in a frying pan, fry the
onion, celery, garlic and green pepper for 3
minutes. Add the curry powder, fry for 1
minute, add the flour and stir until mixed.
Add the milk in a slow steady stream, stirring
constantly until the mixture is thick. Add the
lime juice, salt, ginger and rum. Remove from
the heat. Mix 1 cup of the mixture with the
shrimps. Place ¼ cup shrimp mixture on
each crepe, roll them up and place them in
a buttered baking dish. Pour the remainder
of the sauce over the crepes. Bake in the oven
for 15 – 20 minutes. Garnish with the
reserved shrimps. Serve with mango
chutney.
Serves 5 – 6

Stewed Fish

2 lb (1 kg) shark or firm-fleshed fish, cut
  into 1½" (3 cm) cubes
2 onions, sliced
3 blades of chives, chopped
1 sweet pepper, chopped
1 – 2 tomatoes, chopped
1 tsp dried thyme
2 tbsp lime juice
1 tbsp rum
2 tbsp butter
1 clove garlic, minced
1 tbsp sugar
1 tbsp Worcestershire sauce
⅔ cup fish stock
Salt and pepper to taste

Place the fish in a bowl. Mix the onions,
chives, sweet pepper, tomatoes, thyme, lime
juice and rum together and pour over the
fish. Leave to marinate for 1 hour, turning
frequently.

Melt the butter in a saucepan, add the
garlic and sugar and heat until they *just* begin
to bubble. Fry the fish in the mixture, add
the marinade, Worcestershire sauce, stock
and salt and pepper to taste. Lower the heat,
cover and simmer for 20 minutes. Serve with
lime wedges.
Serves 4

Yesterday's Creole Fish

Any leftover fried fish

Sauce:
2 tbsp butter
1 onion, chopped
½ green pepper, chopped
1 clove garlic, minced
1 16 oz (450 g) tin chopped tomatoes
1 tbsp rum
1 bay leaf
Pinch dried thyme
1 tsp chopped parsley
1 tsp sugar
Salt and pepper to taste

Melt the butter in a medium saucepan, fry the onion and green pepper for 5 minutes. Add the remaining ingredients, bring to the boil, reduce the heat to low and simmer for 20 – 30 minutes.

Preheat the oven to 400°F.

Place the fish in a single layer in an ovenproof dish, spread the sauce evenly over the fish and bake in the oven for 10 – 15 minutes or until it is heated through.

Serves according to amount of fish baked

Shrimps with Rum

*1 lb (450 g) shrimps, shelled and
  deveined*
2 – 3 tbsp olive oil
1 large onion, chopped finely
2 cloves garlic, minced
4 oz (125 g) chopped tomatoes
2 tbsp Cockspur golden rum
Salt and pepper to taste
1 large onion, sliced
¼ cup flour

Heat the oil in a frying pan and lightly fry the onion and garlic until golden but not browned. Add the tomatoes, cook for 2 – 3 minutes. Add the shrimps and fry for 1 minute. Add the rum and ignite. When the flames subside add salt and pepper to taste, cover the pan and cook at a bare simmer for 10 minutes.

Meanwhile, coat the sliced onion with the flour and fry the rings until they are golden and crisp. Drain.

Garnish the shrimps with the onion rings and serve.

Serves 2

STUFFINGS AND VEGETABLES

Glazed Carrots *(left* and West Indian Peas and Rice *(right)*

West Indian Stuffing

½ cup fresh breadcrumbs or cracker
   crumbs
2 tbsp bacon fat or butter
2 tbsp chopped parsley
2 – 3 sprigs thyme
1 large onion, chopped
3 blades chives, chopped
1 tomato, chopped
⅛ tsp black pepper
Small piece hot red pepper, minced
½ tsp salt
2 – 3 tbsp rum

Optional additions:
¼ cup coarsely chopped olives
¼ cup chopped parsley
½ cup frozen green peas

Mix all the ingredients together in a large
bowl.

Quantity:
Use for stuffing chicken, turkey or suckling
pig.

Barbados Rum Fruit Stuffing

¼ cup diced dried apricots
¼ cup raisins
3 – 4 tbsp rum
½ cup water or stock
4 slices white bread
1 large onion, chopped
1 apple, cored and diced
¼ tsp dried thyme
¼ tsp dried sage
1 tsp curry powder
2 tbsp butter
Salt and pepper to taste

Mix together the apricots, raisins, rum and
water or stock in a small saucepan. Bring to
the boil, cover, remove from the heat and
allow to stand for 30 minutes.

Preheat the oven to 375°F.

Cut the bread into small cubes, place on
a baking tray and bake in the oven for 30
minutes. In a medium saucepan, cook the
onion, apple, thyme, sage and curry powder,
with the butter, for 5 minutes over a medium
heat, stirring all the time. Add the apricot and
rum mixture, combine with the bread and
mix well. Season the stuffing with salt and
pepper, to taste. Allow the stuffing to cool
completely before using.

Quantity:
Sufficient for stuffing 1 chicken, can be
doubled for turkey.

Sweet Potato Casserole

4 cups cooked, mashed sweet potatoes
½ cup milk
½ cup butter, melted (separated)
Salt and pepper to taste
½ cup cream
¼ cup rum
¼ tsp freshly grated nutmeg
Grated rind of 1 orange
Chopped walnuts to garnish

Preheat the oven to 350°F.

Mix the sweet potato with the milk and
¼ cup of the butter, season with salt and
pepper to taste. Place in a well-buttered
casserole dish. Mix the cream, rum and nutmeg together, pour over the sweet potato.
Top with a sprinkling of grated orange rind,
then chopped walnuts and dribble with the
remaining butter. Bake in the oven for
30 – 35 minutes.
Serves 4 – 6

Tangy Cauliflower

1 small head of cauliflower, parboiled
⅓ cup mayonnaise
1 tsp prepared mustard
1 very small onion, chopped
1 tsp rum
Grated Cheddar cheese
Paprika

Preheat the oven to 375°F.
    Mix together the mayonnaise, mustard, onion and rum. Pour over the cauliflower, sprinkle with grated cheese, then paprika. Bake in the oven for 20 minutes or until heated through.
Serves 2

Glazed Carrots

1½ lb (750 g) carrots, sliced
2 tbsp butter
¼ cup chicken or beef stock
2 tbsp rum
½ tsp sugar
Salt and pepper to taste
Chopped parsley

Boil the carrots in unsalted water for 3 minutes. Strain the carrots and toss them in the butter until they are coated. Add the stock, rum, sugar, salt and pepper to taste. Cook until the carrots are shiny and tender and the liquid is absorbed. Garnish with parsley and serve.
Serves 6

West Indian Peas and Rice

4 oz (125 g) salt beef or pork, cut into small dice
2 tbsp butter
6 blades chives, chopped
½ tsp dried thyme
½ tsp marjoram
Small piece hot red pepper, minced
1 onion, chopped
2 cloves garlic, minced
1 tbsp Worcestershire sauce
1 tbsp Cockspur golden rum
1 tin green pigeon peas (drained)
1 cup rice
2 cups water
Salt to taste

Soak the salt meat in water to remove excess salt. Fry the meat in the butter with the chives, thyme, marjoram, hot pepper, onion and garlic for about 5 minutes. Add the Worcestershire sauce, rum, peas, rice and water. Adjust seasoning to taste, bring to the boil, cover tightly, reduce the heat and simmer for 20 – 25 minutes or until the rice is cooked and the water is absorbed.
Serves 5

DESSERTS

From the left, Strawberry Mousse Cake, Apricot Delight, Rum Creams, Pineapple Rum Log *(right)* and Chocolate Rum Dessert *(front)*

Strawberry Mousse Cake

1 9" (23 cm) round sponge cake
1 10 oz (300 g) pack frozen strawberries
in syrup, thawed, drained and juice
reserved
1 envelope gelatin (unflavoured)
3 tbsp rum
½ cup granulated sugar
¾ cup heavy whipping cream

Rum syrup:
4 tbsp sugar
3 tbsp water
4 tbsp rum

Make the syrup. Mix together the sugar, water and rum in a small saucepan. Bring to the boil, stirring until the sugar is dissolved. Cool to room temperature.

Make the mousse. In a small saucepan, sprinkle the gelatin over the reserved strawberry syrup, leave to soften for 5 minutes then cook over a low heat, stirring until the gelatin is dissolved. Add the rum. Chop the strawberries coarsely in a blender or food processor, with the sugar. Add the gelatin mixture in a stream and blend until thoroughly mixed. Chill the mixture until it is cold and slightly thickened.

In a chilled bowl whip the cream and fold it into the strawberry mixture.

Assemble the cake. Slice the sponge cake into three equal layers horizontally. Place the bottom sponge layer in a 9" (23 cm) spring form pan, brush with one third of the rum syrup, spread with half the strawberry mousse, top with the second sponge layer. Brush this with one third of the rum syrup, add the remaining strawberry mousse. Brush the cut side of the third layer of sponge cake with the remaining rum syrup and top the mousse with the cake, cut side down. Chill

for several hours. Remove the spring form sides and garnish with rum-flavoured whipped cream.
Serves 8 – 10

Cherry Cream Crown

2 3 oz (100 g) packs ladyfingers
¼ cup rum
8 oz (250 g) cream cheese, at room
temperature
½ cup granulated sugar
2 cups whipping cream
1 tsp vanilla
1 21 oz (650 g) tin cherry pie filling
1 tsp lime juice

Lightly grease the bottom of a 9" (23 cm) spring form pan. Brush the ladyfingers with the rum. Line the sides of the pan with half the ladyfingers, rounded sides out.

In an electric mixer, beat the cream cheese for 1 minute. Gradually add the sugar and continue beating for 1 minute. In a separate bowl beat the cream and vanilla together until stiff.

Fold the cream into the cheese mixture.

Spread half the cheese mixture into the pan, arrange the rest of the ladyfingers over the cheese, top with the remaining cheese mixture, spreading evenly. Refrigerate overnight.

Spread the top of the cheese with the cherry pie filling mixed with the lime juice.
Serves 10

Rummy Oranges (centre), Délice au Chocolat *(bottom, left)*, Rum Cream Torte *(back, right)* and Apricot Bombe *(bottom, right)*

Pineapple Rum Log

1 11 oz (330 g) tin pineapple cubes,
  drained
16 ginger snap biscuits
1 cup whipping cream
2 oz (50 g) milk chocolate, grated
3 tbsp rum
Chocolate curls for decoration

Roughly chop the pineapple cubes. Lay the biscuits flat and sprinkle generously with the rum. Whip the cream until it is thick, reserve two thirds for coating the rolls. To the other third of the cream add the pineapple and grated chocolate. Sandwich the biscuits together, four at a time, with the pineapple cream. Arrange them in stacks, side by side, on a piece of foil and fold tightly. Freeze for 1 hour.

Place the log on a serving dish and coat entirely with the remaining two thirds of the reserved cream. Decorate with chocolate curls.
Serves 6

Rummy Oranges

8 oranges
1 cup granulated sugar
⅔ cup water
¼ cup Cockspur golden rum
¼ cup orange flavoured liqueur

Cut the peel and white pith from the oranges, cut between the membranes to remove segments (work over a bowl to collect any extra juice), squeeze the cores of the oranges and add the liquid to the juice from the orange segments.

Measure the juice and add water to make up to ⅔ cup. Add the sugar to the juice and cook over a medium heat until the sugar is dissolved. Bring the mixture to the boil, and boil, uncovered, for 2 minutes. Allow to cool, then stir in the rum and the liqueur. Pour over the orange segments. Serve well-chilled over ice cream or any of the rum pies, puddings or creams, or use as topping for any of the desserts in this book.
Serves 6 – 8

Macaroon Torte

1 ½ cups finely grated coconut
2 tbsp cornstarch
4 eggs, separated
Pinch cream of tartar
¾ cup granulated sugar
1 tsp vanilla

Topping:
1 ½ cups whipping cream
3 tbsp icing sugar
1 tbsp rum
1 tsp gelatin
2 tbsp rum
1 papaya
   or ½ pineapple
   or 2 mangoes
   or 1 jar stewed guavas
   or a combination of the above fruits
   cut into ¼" (½ cm) cubes
Toasted flaked coconut

Preheat the oven to 400°F.

Sprinkle the 1½ cups coconut into a baking tray and toast for 3 – 4 minutes. Allow to cool. Reduce the oven setting to 325°F.

Grease two 8" (20 cm) cake tins, line them with waxed paper. Grease and flour the paper, set aside.

Mix together the coconut and cornstarch. Beat the egg whites with the cream of tartar to soft peak stage, add ½ cup sugar, 1 tablespoon at a time, beating until glossy. Beat the egg yolks and the remaining sugar for 5 minutes. Add the vanilla. Fold the egg whites into the yolks gently, then fold in the coconut mixture. Divide the mixture into the two tins and bake for 20 minutes. Cool completely. (Cakes will fall in the centre.)

Make the topping. Soften the gelatin in the 2 tablespoons rum, in a basin over hot water. Stir until dissolved. Allow to cool. Whip the cream and icing sugar to soft peaks, add the rum and gelatin mixture.

Gently press the cakes to flatten them, sprinkle with the remaining tablespoon of rum. Spread one cake with some of the whipped cream, then half of the fruit, top with the other cake. Coat the sides and top with the remaining cream and decorate the top with the remaining fruit. Dust the sides of the torte with toasted flaked coconut. Chill for several hours.
Serves 8 – 10

Chocolate Rum Dessert

2 eggs
1 tbsp granulated sugar
½ lb (250 g) butter, melted
½ lb (250 g) chocolate, melted
½ lb (250 g) digestive biscuits, crushed
   in large crumbs
2 tbsp rum
¼ cup chopped walnuts
¼ cup chopped cherries
Whipped cream for decorating

Whisk the eggs and sugar for about 5 minutes, until they are thick and creamy. Slowly add the melted butter, then the melted chocolate, in a thin, steady stream, whisking all the time. Fold in the biscuits, rum, walnuts and cherries. Place in a well-oiled loaf tin, smooth the top and freeze for 4 hours or refrigerate overnight.

Run a knife around the edges and remove from tin. Decorate with whipped cream.
Serves 6 – 8

Flambéd Caramel Custard *(left)*, Annie-Annie's Rum Babas *(back)* and Rum Pie *(front)*

Flambéd Caramel Custard

Caramel:
2 tbsp sugar
2 tbsp water

Custard:
3 eggs
5 tbsp caster sugar
1 ½ cups milk
Generous pinch cinnamon
Thinly pared lime rind, in one piece
Generous ½ cup rum

Make the caramel. Place the ingredients for the caramel in a small, heavy saucepan over a low heat and stir until the sugar is dissolved. Raise the heat to moderate and boil until golden. Remove from heat and pour immediately into 6 individual ramekin moulds.

Make the custard. Preheat the oven to 300°F. Lightly whisk the eggs and sugar together in a medium bowl. Place the milk, cinnamon and lime rind in a medium saucepan over moderate heat and heat until simmering point is reached (just before it boils). Discard the lime rind and slowly stir the mixture into the egg mixture. Pour the mixture evenly into the ramekin dishes, on top of the caramel. Place the dishes in a large baking pan half-filled with boiling water. Carefully place in the oven and bake for 1 hour or until set.

While the caramel custard is still hot, turn out on to serving dishes.

Warm the rum, ignite and pour over the custards, spooning the rum over them until the flames subside. Serve immediately. *Serves 6*

63

Apricot Delight

1 20 oz (600 g) tin apricot halves in
    syrup, drained (reserving ½ cup
liquid)
¼ cup granulated sugar
⅓ cup water
2 tbsp unflavoured gelatin
½ cup Amaretto or apricot flavoured
    liqueur
1 tbsp rum
1½ cups well-chilled whipping cream
Additional whipped cream and apricot
    quarters for garnish

Purée the apricots in a blender or food
processor.

Mix together the sugar with the water,
in a saucepan. Bring to the boil and boil for
3 minutes.

In a small bowl, sprinkle the gelatin over
the liqueur to soften; leave for 5 minutes.
Add the gelatin mixture to the hot syrup and
stir until the gelatin is dissolved. Cool for 5
minutes. Add the apricot purée and the rum,
let the mixture cool to room temperature.

Whip the cream to stiff peaks and gently
fold into the apricot mixture.

Rinse a mould with cold water; do not
dry it. Put the apricot mixture into the mould
and refrigerate for at least 6 hours. Turn out
of the mould and garnish with additional
cream and apricot quarters if desired.
Serves 8 – 10

Peach Delight

As above but substitute peaches for the
apricots.

Chocolate Mocha Mousse

4 oz (125 g) semi-sweet chocolate,
    chopped coarsely
¼ cup strong black coffee
4 eggs, separated
1 tbsp butter
1 tbsp rum
Cream for garnish

Melt the chocolate in the coffee in a pan, over
medium heat, stirring until the chocolate is
thick and creamy. Remove from the heat and
beat in the egg yolks, one at a time, to thicken
the mixture. Beat in the butter and rum.
Allow to cool slightly.

Whip the egg whites in a separate bowl
until they are stiff. Gently fold the egg whites
into the cooled chocolate mixture. Place in
a bowl and chill for at least 6 hours or
overnight. Garnish with whipped cream.
Serves 6

Rum-flavoured Whipped Cream

1 cup whipping cream
1 tbsp icing sugar
2 tbsp rum

Whip the cream to soft peaks, add the sugar
and rum, continue whipping until stiff.

Grand Marnier and Rum Puddings *(left)*, Rum Puddings *(centre, back)*, Chocolate Mocha Mousse *(centre, front)* and Cherry Cream Crown *(right)*

Grand Marnier and Rum Pudding

2 large eggs, at room temperature
⅔ cup sugar
3 tbsp strong brewed coffee, cooled
2 tbsp Grand Marnier or other orange
* flavoured liqueur*
2 tbsp rum
3 8 oz (250 g) packs cream cheese, cut
* into small pieces, at room temperature*
Whipped cream, finely shredded orange
* rind, fresh mint leaves for garnish*

Combine the eggs and sugar in a blender or food processor for 1 minute. Add the coffee, liqueur and rum, blend for 20 seconds. With the machine running, add the cream cheese and blend until smooth.

Divide the mixture amongst 8 wine glasses, cover with film wrap and refrigerate overnight. Top each with whipped cream, orange rind and a mint leaf.

Can also be served with **Rummy Oranges** (recipe on page 61) or any tropical fruit available. Excellent with stewed guavas.
Serves 8

Délice au Chocolat

¾ lb (350 g) semi-sweet chocolate,
* chopped coarsely*
3 tbsp coffee liqueur
1 tbsp Cockspur golden rum
7 egg yolks, at room temperature
½ lb (250 g) butter, cut into 16 pieces

Butter a 3-cup mould. Melt the chocolate in the liqueur and rum in a double boiler, over simmering water. Whisk the egg yolks in, one at a time. Whisk in 10 pieces of butter, 2 at a time, and then whisk in the remaining butter. Pour into the prepared mould and chill for at least 6 hours. This can be prepared at least two days in advance.

Just before serving, place the mould in a pan of hot water for 30 seconds, run a knife around the edges and turn out. Serve with **Rum-flavoured Whipped Cream** (recipe on page 64). Cut into very thin slices to serve.
Serves 8 – 10

Fruit Dip or Topping

1 cup sour cream
1 cup whipped cream
4 tbsp brown sugar
1 tbsp rum
1 tbsp orange flavoured liqueur
Freshly grated nutmeg

Mix the sour cream, cream, sugar, rum and liqueur together. Pour into a dip bowl, sprinkle with nutmeg. Serve with sliced tropical fruit or as a topping to desserts.
Makes 2 cups of dip

Apricot Bombe

2 1½ oz (45 g) sachets dessert topping mix
1 cup cold milk
2 tbsp granulated sugar
2 oz (50 g) milk chocolate, melted
1 15 oz (450 g) tin apricots, drained
2 tsp rum
½ tsp grated orange rind
2 tbsp orange juice

Make up one sachet of topping mix, using half a cup of milk. Whisk in 1 tablespoon of the sugar and the melted chocolate.

Line the base and sides of a 2 lb (1 kg) shatterproof pudding bowl with the mixture and freeze until solid.

Meanwhile, mix the apricots, in a blender or food processor, with the rum, orange rind and juice.

Make up the second sachet of topping with the rest of the milk and sugar. Fold in the apricot mixture and spoon into the centre of the frozen chocolate cream.

Freeze for 8 hours or overnight. Dip the basin in warm water and turn out to serve.
Serves 6

Peach Bombe

As above but substitute peaches for the apricots.

Rum Cream Torte

8½ oz (250 g) pack chocolate cookies
½ cup butter, melted
1 envelope unflavoured gelatin
⅓ cup cold water
⅓ cup rum
6 egg yolks
1 cup granulated sugar
2 cups well-chilled whipping cream
Fresh fruit as desired

Finely crush the cookies in a blender or food processor, add the butter and process in short bursts, until the mixture begins to gather together. Press the crumbs into a 9″ (23 cm) spring form pan.

Sprinkle the gelatin over the cold water in a small bowl, place in a pan of simmering water and stir until dissolved. Add the rum to the gelatin and cool slightly, stirring occasionally. Beat the egg yolks in an electric mixer for about 5 minutes, until they are pale yellow. Gradually add the sugar and continue beating until the mixture is thick.

Using clean beaters and a separate bowl, beat the cream to soft peaks, Stir the gelatin into the egg yolk mixture then fold in the cream. Pour into the crust and freeze for at least 6 hours or overnight. Arrange fruit on top if desired, and serve.
Serves 8

Rum Cream

3 egg yolks
¼ cup granulated sugar
1 tbsp lime juice
3 tbsp rum
1 cup thick cream, whipped
Additional whipped cream for garnish

Beat the egg yolks, sugar and lime juice for about 5 minutes, until thick and lemon-coloured. Add the rum in a slow stream. Fold in the whipped cream. Spoon into 4 stemmed glasses and chill for at least 4 hours. Garnish with additional whipped cream.
Serves 4

Rum Pie

1 ready prepared and baked Graham
*   cracker 9" (23 cm) pie crust*
1½ tsp gelatin
2 tbsp water
2 eggs, separated
½ cup evaporated milk
¼ cup sugar
¼ tsp salt
⅓ cup light corn syrup
6 tbsp rum (separated)
1 cup thick cream
3 tbsp icing sugar

Sprinkle the gelatin over the water and leave to soften for 10 minutes.

In a small saucepan combine the egg yolks, evaporated milk, sugar and salt. Cook over a moderately low heat, stirring until it is thick enough to coat a spoon but do not let it boil. Remove the pan from the heat, stir in the softened gelatin until it dissolves.

Allow the mixture to cool completely. In a medium bowl, beat the egg whites into soft peaks, slowly add the corn syrup and continue beating for 10 minutes. Beat in 4 tablespoons of rum and fold into the yolk mixture. Pour into the pie crust and chill for 1 hour.

Whip the cream with the icing sugar into soft peaks, add 2 tablespoons of rum and whip until blended. Cover the pie with the cream and chill for a further 4 hours.
Serves 8

Rum Pudding

4 egg yolks
½ cup granulated sugar
⅓ cup rum
1 tbsp gelatin
⅔ cup milk
2 cups thick cream

In the bowl of a double boiler, beat the egg yolks with the sugar, place the bowl over a pan of simmering water and whisk the yolk mixture until it is thick and lukewarm. Transfer the mixture to a bowl and whisk with an electric mixer for about 5 minutes, until it is very thick. Add the rum in a slow, steady stream.

In a small saucepan sprinkle the gelatin over the milk to soften; leave for about 5 minutes. Cook over a low heat until the gelatin dissolves. Place the milk over crushed ice and chill, stirring often until it thickens. Stir into the yolk mixture.

Whip the cream and fold this into the yolk mixture. Spoon into 8 goblets and chill for at least 4 hours. Serve with fruit in season.
Serves 8

Caribbean Bananas

¾ *cup flaked coconut*
3 *tbsp butter*
½ *cup brown sugar*
1 *cup rum*
½ *tsp ground cinnamon*
8 *bananas, peeled and sliced*
Vanilla ice cream or coconut ice cream

Heat the coconut in a large frying pan or grill until toasted. Remove from the pan and set aside to cool.

Add the butter, sugar, rum and cinnamon to the pan and heat until the mixture bubbles. Add the bananas and cook until heated through.

Spoon the ice cream into dishes, spoon the hot banana mixture over the ice cream. Sprinkle with the toasted coconut and serve immediately.
Serves 8

Flambéd Tropical Banana Splits

4 *tbsp butter*
¼ *cup shredded coconut*
¼ *cup brown sugar*
½ *tsp cinnamon*
1 8 oz (250 g) tin sliced peaches or
  mangoes (drained)
2 *bananas, split lengthwise*
*Chocolate, vanilla and strawberry ice
  creams*
¼ *cup rum*
Marachino cherries

Melt the butter in a thick pan, add the coconut, stir and cook over a medium heat until toasted. Remove the coconut, keeping some of the butter in the pan. Stir the brown sugar and cinnamon into the pan, add the peaches or mangoes and heat through.

Line two banana split dishes with the banana halves, place one scoop of each ice cream in each dish. Return the peach mixture to the heat, add rum and ignite. Spoon the peach mixture over the banana splits, sprinkle with the coconut and garnish with the cherries.
Serves 2

Banana Rum Crisp

4 *firm bananas, peeled and sliced*
2 *tsp lime juice*
2 *tbsp butter*
1 ¼ *cups rum*
6 *tbsp brown sugar*
¼ *tsp grated nutmeg*
¾ *tsp ground cinnamon*
Finely grated rind of ½ orange
1 *cup vanilla wafer crumbs*
½ *cup chopped nuts*
2 *tsp white sugar*

Preheat the oven to 375°F.

Sprinkle the bananas with the lime juice, place in a well-buttered pie dish. Mix 1 cup of the rum with the brown sugar, nutmeg, cinnamon and orange rind. Pour over the bananas. Mix the vanilla wafer crumbs and nuts together and sprinkle over the bananas. Bake in the oven for 20 minutes. Just before serving, warm the sugar and the remaining ¼ cup of rum, set alight and pour over the pie.
Serves 4

Annie-Annie's Rum Babas

⅔ *cup currants or raisins*
¾ *cup Cockspur golden rum*
3 tbsp lukewarm water
1 tbsp or 1 pack yeast
4 eggs
1 tsp salt
1 tbsp sugar
1¾ cup flour
½ cup butter, softened

Sugar syrup:
2½ cups sugar
4 cups water

Soak the fruit in the rum for 20 minutes. Drain the fruit, reserving the rum. Soak the yeast in the lukewarm water for 5 minutes. Add the eggs, salt and sugar to the yeast mixture. Place the flour in the food processor, turn on the machine and add the yeast mixture through the chute. Process for 2 minutes. Leave the mixture in the food processor bowl, with a cover over it, and allow it to rise for 45 minutes to 1 hour. Remove the cover, add the butter and process for 1 minute. Stir in the fruit. Put the mixture, in heaped tablespoonfuls, into well-greased muffin tins. Cover with a cloth and allow to rise for 45 minutes to 1 hour. Bake in the oven, preheated to 400°F, for 20 – 25 minutes.

Meanwhile, prepare the syrup by boiling the sugar and water until the sugar is dissolved. Boil for 3 – 4 minutes longer. Remove from heat and add the reserved rum. While the babas are still warm, place into the syrup, a few at a time, turning until they swell. Continue until all babas are coated. Sprinkle with additional rum and serve.
Makes 16 – 20 babas

CAKES, PASTRIES AND SAUCES

Laurel-Ann's Wedding Cake with Hard Rum Sauce

Laurel-Ann's Wedding Cake or Christmas Cake West Indian Style

Fruit mixture:
1 cup raisins
1 cup currants
½ cup candied cherries
½ cup candied citrus peel
1 cup mixed dried fruit
1 cup rum
1 cup sweet sherry or port wine
½ cup brandy

Cake:
½ lb (450 g) butter, at room
*   temperature*
½ cup brown sugar
4 eggs
2 cups flour
1 tsp baking powder
1 tsp ground ginger
1 tsp ground nutmeg
3 tsp ground cinnamon
½ tsp ground cloves
½ tsp ground allspice
2½ tsp lemon essence
2½ tsp almond essence
1 tsp vanilla essence
¼ – ½ cup brown food colouring
½ cup rum
Additional rum for basting during
*   storage*

Fruit mixture:
Mix together all the ingredients and store in a tightly sealed jar for at least 1 month.

The cake:
Prepare a 10″ (25 cm) deep round cake baking tin or a 13″ × 9″ (33 cm × 23 cm) baking tin by lining it with two layers of waxed paper, greasing between the layers.

Preheat the oven to 250°F.

In a large bowl, cream together the butter and sugar until they are light and fluffy. Add the eggs, one at a time, mixing well after each addition.

Sift the flour, baking powder and all the dry spices together. Add the lemon essence, almond essence and vanilla essence to the fruit mixture.

By hand, stir tablespoonfuls of the flour mixture and the fruit mixture, alternately, into the butter, sugar and egg mixture.

Add the browning gradually, stirring until a deepish brown colour is reached.

Turn the cake mixture into the baking tin, smooth the top and bake in the oven for 3 – 4 hours or until a skewer or wooden toothpick, inserted, comes out clean. This can take an additional hour or two.

Remove the cake from the oven, prick it all over with a skewer or toothpick and pour the rum all over it.

Remove the cake from the tin when it is cool, wrap it tightly in waxed paper, place it in an airtight container and leave for a month for best flavour. Every week, prick the cake with a skewer and pour on about 1 tbsp of rum.
Makes one 5 lb (2½ kg) cake (approx)

Hard Rum Sauce

⅓ cup butter, at room temperature
1 cup icing sugar
4 – 5 tbsp rum

Cream the butter, gradually add the icing sugar, beat until light and fluffy. Slowly beat in the rum in a thin stream. Serve with any steamed pudding.

Excellent with **Christmas Cake West Indian Style** (recipe on this page).

Rum Cake

1 cup butter
1 ½ cups white sugar
4 eggs
1 lime (grated peel and juice)
1 ½ cups sifted flour
1 cup cornstarch
2 tsp baking powder
¼ cup Cockspur golden rum

Preheat the oven to 350°F.

In a large bowl, cream the butter until it is light, gradually add the sugar and beat until fluffy. Add the eggs, unbeaten, one at a time. Beat well after each addition. Add the juice and peel of the lime.

Sift the flour, cornstarch and baking powder together. Add to the butter mixture alternately with the rum. Beat well and pour into a well-greased tube pan or cake tin. Bake for 1 ¼ hours, or until cooked.

Turn the cake out, upside down, on a rack and leave to cool. Frost with any orange frosting.

Rum Spice Cake

1 cup raisins
4 heaped tbsp butter, at room
    temperature
4 heaped tbsp sugar
1 whole egg plus 1 egg yolk (reserve
    white for glaze)
1 cup flour
½ tsp nutmeg
½ tsp cinnamon
¼ tsp ground cloves
1 tsp baking powder
3 tbsp rum

Glaze:
10 oz (250 g) icing sugar
2 tsp rum
Reserved egg white (see above)

Preheat the oven to 350°F.

Boil the raisins for 5 minutes. Drain. In a large bowl, cream the butter and sugar until light and fluffy, add the unbeaten egg plus the yolk and beat until well combined. Sift the flour with the nutmeg, cinnamon, cloves and baking powder. Add the flour mixture to the butter mixture alternately with the rum. Stir in the raisins.

Place in a well-greased 8″ (20 cm) baking tin and bake in the oven for 1 hour. Turn out, cool and glaze.

To make the glaze:
Mix the egg white and icing sugar together, beat until they are stiff. Slowly add the rum.

Rum Sauce

½ cup white sugar
1 tbsp cornstarch
½ tsp ground cinnamon
Pinch salt
½ cup water
½ cup rum
1 tbsp lime juice
2 tbsp butter

Mix the sugar, cornstarch, cinnamon and salt to a smooth paste with a little of the water. Gradually add the rest of the water, the rum and the lime juice. Cook the mixture, stirring constantly, until it thickens. Remove from heat and stir in the butter.

Excellent with desserts or poured over ice cream.

Pina Colada Bread *(left)*, Rum Cake *(back)* and Chocolate Rum Balls *(front)*

Chocolate Rum Balls

1 6 oz (180 g) pack chocolate chips
  (1 cup)
⅓ cup rum
3 tbsp light corn syrup
2½ cups vanilla or chocolate cookie
  crumbs
1 cup chopped pecan nuts or walnuts
½ cup icing sugar
Granulated sugar

In a small saucepan, combine the chocolate chips, rum and corn syrup. Cook over a low heat until the chocolate melts. In a large bowl, mix together the cookie crumbs, nuts and icing sugar, add the chocolate mixture and stir thoroughly. Let the mixture rest for 30 minutes.

Shape into 1″ (2½ cm) balls, roll in granulated sugar until well coated. Allow to season in an airtight container for two days.
Makes 36 balls

Rum-Berry Sauce

½ lb (225 g) fresh or frozen cranberries
½ cup orange juice (fresh)
6 tbsp sugar
1 tsp grated orange rind
3 tbsp rum
1 tbsp butter
Pinch of salt

Pick over the cranberries, place them in a saucepan with the orange juice, sugar and orange rind. Bring to the boil, reduce the heat and simmer for 10 minutes or until the cranberries burst open.

Remove from the heat, stir in the rum, butter and salt. Serve warm or cold over ice cream or steamed puddings.

Pina Colada Pancakes

2 cups flour
2 tbsp baking powder
¼ cup sugar
½ tsp salt
1 15 oz (800 g) can crushed pineapple,
  drained, reserving syrup
1 cup milk plus additional milk
2 eggs, beaten
¼ cup melted butter
1 cup flaked toasted coconut, divided
  ¾ cup and ¼ cup

Fluffy rum sauce:
4 egg yolks
1¼ cups icing sugar
¼ cup rum
2 tbsp frozen whipped topping

Make the sauce. Beat the egg yolks with an electric mixer on high speed until thick, about 5 minutes. Slowly add the icing sugar and continue beating until the mixture is combined. Gradually add the rum, beating until blended. Fold in the whipped cream and refrigerate until serving time.

Make the pancakes. In a large bowl, mix the flour, baking powder, sugar and salt. Drain the pineapple, reserving the juice. Add enough milk to the reserved juice to make up to 2 cups. Combine the juice and milk with the eggs and butter, add to the flour mixture and mix until just combined.

In a small bowl, mix the pineapple with ¾ cup of the toasted coconut.

Preheat the griddle and oil it lightly. Pour the pancake batter, ¼ cup at a time, onto the griddle. Sprinkle the pancake with some of the pineapple and coconut mixture and cook until bubbles begin to appear. Turn the pancake over and cook until done. Serve

hot with fluffy rum sauce, sprinkled with the reserved coconut.
Makes 10 – 12 pancakes

Banana Rum Cake

Cake:
2 large overripe bananas, mashed
4 tbsp sour cream
2 tbsp rum
3 eggs
3 oz (75 g) granulated sugar
8 oz (250 g) flour
2 oz (50 g) butter, melted

Rum syrup:
½ cup water
4 tsp lime juice
4 oz (125 g) granulated sugar
2 tbsp rum

Preheat the over to 400°F.

Make the cake. Mix together the bananas, sour cream and the rum. Whisk the eggs and sugar together for 5 minutes. Fold in the flour, then the melted butter and then the banana mixture. Pour into a well greased 9″ (23 cm) round tin. Bake in the oven for 40 – 45 minutes or until the cake is done.

Meanwhile, make the rum syrup. Put the water, lime juice and sugar in a saucepan and bring to the boil. Reduce the heat and simmer for 10 minutes, stirring occasionally to dissolve the sugar. Remove from the heat and stir in the rum.

When the cake is cooked, turn it out onto a rack, prick it all over with a skewer while it is still warm, and spoon over the rum syrup.

Banana Daiquiri Bread

2 cups flour
1 tsp baking powder
¼ tsp baking soda
½ tsp salt
½ tsp nutmeg
½ tsp cinnamon
½ cup butter, room temperature
¾ cup sugar
¾ cup puréed ripe banana
2 eggs, at room temperature
⅓ cup rum
2 tbsp lime juice
½ tsp rum extract or lemon extract
½ cup chopped almonds

Grease an 8″ × 4″ (20 cm × 10 cm) or 9″ × 5″ (23 cm × 13 cm) loaf tin. Preheat the oven to 350°F.

In a large bowl, mix the flour, baking powder, soda, salt, nutmeg and cinnamon. Leave to one side.

In a medium bowl, cream the butter, gradually add the sugar, beat for 1 minute until the mixture is light and airy. Add the banana, eggs, rum, lime juice and extract, beat until blended. Stir into the flour mixture until the dry ingredients are *just barely* moistened. *Do not overmix.* Stir in the nuts, place in the prepared loaf tin, smooth the top and bake for 55 – 60 minutes, or until a skewer or wooden toothpick, inserted, comes out clean. Let the loaf stand in the tin for 10 minutes, then turn it out on to a rack and leave to cool.
Makes 1 loaf

Rum Tea Biscuits

1½ cups flour
1 tsp baking powder
½ tsp salt
2 tbsp sugar
½ cup cold butter, cut into 8 pieces
⅓ cup plus 1 tbsp rum
⅓ cup currants

Rum glaze:
1 tbsp melted butter
2 tsp sugar
1 tsp rum

Make the rum glaze. In a small saucepan, combine the butter and sugar. Add the rum and cook gently, stirring all the time, until the sugar has dissolved. Leave to cool.

Preheat the oven to 400°F.

Make the biscuits. In a large bowl, mix the flour, baking powder, salt and sugar. Using a pastry blender or two knives, cut in the butter until the mixture resembles very coarse crumbs. Add the rum and currants, stirring until the mixture just holds together. Knead gently 12 times.

Pat or roll out the dough to ½″ (1 cm) thickness, cut out the biscuits with a 2″ (5 cm) cutter and place them on an ungreased baking sheet 1½″ (4 cm) apart. Brush with the rum glaze and bake for 6 – 8 minutes or until lightly browned.
Makes 24 biscuits

Rum Sauce on Ice Cream *(left and right)* and Rum Brownies *(centre)*

Rum Brownies

½ cup of butter
6 tbsp unsweetened cocoa powder
¾ cup flour
¼ tsp baking powder
Pinch of salt
2 large eggs, beaten lightly
¾ cup sugar
4 tbsp Cockspur golden rum
1 tsp vanilla
1 cup chopped nuts

Frosting:
4 tbsp unsweetened cocoa powder
1 tbsp melted butter
1 cup icing sugar
3 tbsp Cockspur golden rum

Preheat the oven to 350°F.

Melt the butter in a heavy saucepan, add the cocoa and stir until mixed. Sift the flour, baking powder and pinch of salt together in a medium bowl. In a small bowl, beat the eggs and sugar together for 5 minutes, add the rum and vanilla. Mix in the flour mixture with the cocoa mixture then add the nuts and place in a well greased 8″ (20 cm) square baking pan. Bake in the oven for 30 minutes. Leave to cool.

Make the frosting. Beat the cocoa, melted butter and icing sugar well together. Add the rum. Use to frost the cooled brownies.
Makes 16 brownies.

Pina Colada Bread

1 ½ cups shredded coconut, divided
  1 ¼ cups and ¼ cup
2 ¾ cups flour
2 tsp baking powder
½ tsp baking soda
1 tsp salt
¾ cup sugar
1 egg, at room temperature
1 cup unsweetened pineapple juice, at
  room temperature
½ cup rum
1 tsp vanilla essence
2 tbsp vegetable oil

Pineapple rum glaze:
3 tbsp butter
2 tbsp pineapple juice
½ cup sugar
¼ cup rum

Make the pineapple rum glaze. In a small saucepan, combine the butter, pineapple juice and sugar. Bring to the boil and boil for 5 minutes. Add the rum and leave to cool.

Make the bread. Generously grease a 9″ × 5″ (23 cm × 13 cm) loaf tin. Preheat the oven to 350°F.

Spread the coconut on a baking sheet and bake for 4 – 6 minutes, stirring frequently, until it is golden brown. Leave to cool.

In a large bowl, mix the flour, baking powder, soda, salt, sugar and 1 ¼ cups of the toasted coconut. (Reserve ¼ cup for topping.)

In a medium bowl, lightly beat the egg, stir in the pineapple juice, rum, vanilla and oil. Stir into the flour mixture until *just* combined. *Do not overmix.*

Place in the prepared baking tin, smooth the top and bake for 55 – 60 minutes or until a skewer or wooden toothpick, inserted, comes out clean. Let the loaf stand in the tin for 10 minutes, then turn it out onto a rack. While it is still warm, prick it all over with a skewer and pour over the rum glaze. Sprinkle with the reserved coconut and leave to cool.

Makes 1 loaf

INDEX

Numbers in *italics* refer to illustrations

Ali's Chicken 26
Annie-Annie's Rum Babas *63*, 69
Apricto Bombe *61*, 66
Apricot Delight *59*, 64

Bajan seasoning 51
Banana Daiquiri Bread 76
Banana Rum Cake 75
Banana Rum Crisp 68
Banana-Rum Fish, Dad's 50
Banana Split, Flambéd 68
Bananas, Caribbean 68
Barbados Party Chicken Pelao 30, *31*
Barbecue Sauce, Rum 17
Barbecue Steaks, Marinated 34
Barbecued Fish with Rum-Ginger Sauce *47*, 48
Barbecued Fish Steaks, Marinated 48
barbecuing/broiling
    beef/lamb 34, 35
    fish 48, 50
    pork 40-42, 44, 45
    poultry 24, 29, 30
Battered Fried Fish *49*, 49
beef *33*, 34-8
Beef Kidneys 34, *35*
broiling: *see* barbecuing

cakes *71*-5
Caramel Custard, Flambéd *63*, 63

Caribbean Bananas 68
Caribbean Chicken Legs 29
Caribbean Pork Tenderloin, *39* 46
Carrot Soup 17
Carrots, Glazed *55*, 57
Cauliflower, Tangy 57
Cheddar-Rum Raisin Spread *15*, 16
Cherry Cream Crown 60, *65*
chicken 16, *27-31*
Chicken Legs, Caribbean 29
Chicken Wings with Rum Barbecue Sauce 16
Chocolat, Délice au 65
Chocolate Mocha Mousse 64, *65*
Chocolate Rum Balls *74*, 74
Chocolate Rum Dessert *59*, 62
Christmas Cake West Indian Style *71*, 72
Coconut Punch 12, *13, 15*
Coffee, Mexican 12
Creole Fish, Yesterday's 53
crêpes *23*, 28, *49*, 52
Curried Chicken 27
Curried Shrimp Crêpes *51*, 52

Délice au Chocolat 65
desserts *59-69*
drinks 12-14
Drumettes, Soy-Honey 16
duck *20*, 21

Egg Nog, Orange 14
Egg Nog *15*
Fettucine and Chicken 25

fish *47*-53
Fried Spiced Chicken 22, *23*
Fruit Dip 66
Fruit Topping 66
Fruited Chicken 26
Frying
    fish 49, 51, 53
    pork 43
    poultry 22

Goose, Roast 22
Grand Marnier and Rum Pudding *65*, 65
Grilled Chicken, Tangy 24

Ham Slices, Buffet 42
Hawaiian Chicken 29
Hawaiian Pork Roast 40
Hot Rum Mocha 13

kebabs *33*, 35, *40*, 41, *47*, 50
kidneys 35

Lamb Kebabs *33*, 35
Laurel-Ann's Wedding Cake, with Hard Rum Sauce *71*, 72

Macaroon Torte *61*, 62
Mexican Coffee 12
Molasses Rum Glazed Pork 45
mousses *59*, 60, 64, *65*
Mushroom Veal Cordon-Bleu 37
Mustard Sauced Fish 49

Olive Beef Casserole 37
Olive Chicken Casserole *20*, 21
Olive Duck Casserole *20*, 21
Orange Chicken *25*, 28

Orange Gingered Fish 48
Orange Sauce 39
Oriental Hoisin Chicken 30
Oxtail Stew 35

Papika Chicken 21
Paprika Duck 21
Party Punch 11, 12
pasta 25
Peach Bombe 66
Peach Delight 64
Peas and Rice, West Indian 57
Pelao, Simple 30
Pepper Broiled Fish 50
Pina Colada Bread 74, 78
Pina Colada Pancakes 75
Pineapple, Grilled 29
Pineapple Chicken with
  Yellow Rice 19, 23
Pineapple Rum Log 59, 61
Ponche Crema 12
Poor Man's Liqueur 13
pork 39-46
Pork, Molasses Rum Glazed 45
Pork Chops, Honeyed 44
Pork Kebabs, Spicy Orange 40,
  41
Pork Loin, Rolled, with Rum
  Curry Glaze 20
Pork Roast 44, 45
  Hawaiian 40, 41
  Orange Sauced 39, 46
Pork Strips, Fried, with
  Scallion Sauce 43
Pork Tenderloin, Caribbean 46
Punch 11, 12, 13, 14, 15

rice 24, 30, 57
Rice, Yellow 24
roasting
  pork 20, 40, 42-46
  poultry 20, 22

rum, history of 7
Rum Babas, Annie-Annie's
  63, 69
Rum Barbecue Sauce 17
Rum Brownies 77, 77
Rum Cake 73, 74
Rum Chilli 33, 36
Rum Cream Torte 66
Rum creams 59, 67
Rum Curried Chicken Crêpes
  23, 28
Rum Fried Fish 51, 51
Rum and Fruit Stuffing 56
Rum Glaze 76
Rum Mustard Glazed Ham 42
Rum-Nut Brie 15, 16
Rum Pie 63, 67
Rum Pudding 67
Rum Punch Chicken 27
Rum Sauce 73
  Fluffy 75
  Hard 71, 72
  on Ice Cream 77
Rum Spice Cake 73
Rum Syrup 60, 75
Rum Tea Biscuits 76
Rum-Berry Sauce 74
Rum-flavoured Whipped
  Cream 64
Rummy Oranges 61, 61

Sauce
  Barbecue Rum 16, 17
  Mustard 49
  Orange 39
  Rum 71, 72, 73, 75, 77
  Rum-Berry 74
  Rum-Ginger 47, 48
  Scallion 43
SDQ Chicken à la Judsy 22
Seasoning Bajan 51

Shrimp Crêpes, Curried 51, 52
Shrimp Kebabs, 47, 50
Shrimps with Rum 53
soups 17
Spareribs
  Caribbean 39, 40
  Lime 42
  Oriental 45
  Simple 9, 41, 42
Spiced Milk Punch 14
starters 16-17
Stewed Fish 51, 52
stewing
  beef 35-37
  fish 52, 53
  poultry 21, 23, 26, 27
Sticky Chicken 23, 26
Strawberry Mousse Cake 59,
  60
stuffing 56
Suckling Pig, Stuffed 43
Sweet Potato Casserole 56

Tangy Cauliflower 57
Tangy Grilled Chicken 24
Turkey Breast with Rum Curry
  Glaze 20

Veal, Mushroom Cordon-Bleu
  37
vegetables 56-7
Wedding Cake, Laurel Ann's
  with Hard Rum Sauce 7172
West Indian Beef Stew 33, 36
West Indian Peas and Rice 55,
  57
West Indian Stuffing 56
West Indian Style Christmas
  Cake 71, 72

Yellow Split Pea Soup 17